THE LAST POEMS OF PHILIP FRENEAU

The Last Poems of
PHILIP FRENEAU

Edited by LEWIS LEARY

GREENWOOD PRESS, PUBLISHERS
WESTPORT, CONNECTICUT

Contents

Introduction

PHILIP FRENEAU retired from active participation in public affairs as a journalist in 1800. For twenty-five years—with one interlude just after the close of the American Revolution—he had been active in defense of personal and national liberties. He had not been successful in a worldly sense. He had failed in one after another of his attempts to found a periodical publication which could be a mouthpiece for the aspirations and achievement of the American common man. He had made enemies. Too quick to snap in anger at whatever seemed to him an abuse of privilege, he had struck blindly and often without practical foresight. Washington, Adams, and Hamilton had each felt the flick of his knotted satirical whip. Now, however, to him the battle must have seemed over. The forces of reaction were in retreat. Jefferson had been elected as President of the United States. In spite of a bitterness undoubtedly engendered by his own personal failure, Freneau must have been glad to lay his pen aside and retire to his Monmouth County farm in New Jersey.

"I think," he later confided to his friend James Madison, "after the age of fifty or thereabouts, the vanity of authorship ought to cease." But vanity aside, Freneau had to keep on writing: "Every day of my life convinces me," he wrote from his retirement, "that while I live I must be active." So during the opening years of the nineteenth century he contributed an occasional poem or article to the newspapers of New York, Philadelphia, or Charleston. He collected his verse into a two-volume edition in 1809 and, again, when the War of 1812 had given new lease to his belligerent muse, in 1815. Neither was totally successful. Each was attacked by political opponents, not as poetry but as partisan propaganda. But such small adversities as lack of critical acclaim had never completely defeated Philip Freneau. Inspired by a visit to Dr. David Hosack's botanical experiments in New York, he planned a long poem after the manner of Erasmus Darwin's *The Botanic Garden*. Again inspired by the repulse of the British at New Orleans, he composed fourteen hundred lines in heroic measure to celebrate the American victory. Neither poem was published, if indeed the former was ever completed, and trace of neither has been found among the poet's scanty literary remains. Both, we suspect, were derivative from Freneau's favorite classic models of the eighteenth century, for certainly we should not expect from a veteran of sixty-four the agility necessary to keep pace with changing literary styles.

In diction and in spirit Freneau already represented a time that was past. To his more progressive neighbors in Monmouth County he must even have seemed a strange old man. Slightly stooped, but wiry, with deep-set grey eyes which when he spoke flashed brightly to relieve the habitual melancholy of his expression, he scorned innovation in dress or in deportment. Proudly wearing his own grey hair, he ridiculed those among his contemporaries who sported the more fashionable—"foppish" was his word—tye-wig. He was known as an opinionated gaffer who scorned display, who wore "small-clothes" and cocked hat as long as he lived, and who would neither eat nor drink nor wear anything not of domestic origin. And so with his verse. It was of an era now past, in an idiom already strangely out of place beside the smooth and modern phrases of Fitz-Greene Halleck and Rodman Drake. His was a more stark and didactic poetry, founded on principles of order and of human justice, clothed with none of the easy sentimentality which Tom Moore early in the new century had helped make popular in America. It was poetry of domestic origin, founded on what Freneau felt were distinctively American notions of freedom, built solidly on foundations of rational common sense. The subject might be slight—a lone apple hanging on a tree, a thoughtless woman, or, as had so often been the wont of Freneau's earlier contemporaries, a lonely tomb—but the tone was serious and corrective. No lilt of line or pretty patter of phrase ever disguised the poet's utilitarian purpose, to chasten and improve.

When in 1822, at the age of seventy, Freneau made plans to publish a final, "new, correct, and elegant edition" of his writings, he had already on hand a batch of poems never collected in a volume. Some of them had appeared six years before in the *Weekly Museum* in New York; a few had been printed in a Trenton newspaper during the past twelve months. But most of them had never been in print in any form. Many of them were really new, the enthusiastic reactions to contemporary events of an old man who gloried in the conviction that his mind could remain "young to all Eternity." Others were older poems which he had kept by him for a long time, for correction or expansion we suppose, before giving them to the public. As soon as it became evident to Freneau that his projected new volume would not appear in an America which seemed at the time to furnish no market for the products of domestic talent, he apparently determined to publish them through another medium. Therefore, during the next two years he contributed a succession of poems to the *True American* in Trenton and to the *Fredonian* in New Brunswick. Sometimes a poem appeared in one newspaper first, sometimes in another: most of them appeared in both, but often in slightly different form, sometimes with a different title, and almost invariably with a different signature. It must have been, in one sense, a literary house-cleaning, the effort of an old man of letters to get his professional affairs in order. In another sense, perhaps, it represents the determination of a man still vigorous, who, though often disappointed in his literary projects, never had and never would acknowledge defeat. True to a life-long principle of semi-anonymity, he simply signed most of them with one of the symbols "F," "R," "E," "N," "A," or "U."

I have elsewhere shown in some detail the links in the investigative chain which bind these poems surely to Freneau.[1] The purpose of the present volume is to bring together those poems known to be Freneau's which were either written or for the first time printed during the period extending from the publication of his last collected edition in 1815 to his death in 1832. The earliest of them appeared in 1816, the latest is in a manuscript dated 1827—from Freneau's sixty-fourth to his seventy-fifth year. These poems are herein printed in the order of their first appearance. Many of them, however, were reprinted once, sometimes twice, each time in a form slightly different from the one before. In these instances I have generally reproduced the form of the latest version. But even at seventy Freneau still tinkered with the phraseology and rime schemes of his verses, experimenting with emendations which, we are led to believe from

[1] *That Rascal Freneau: A Study in Literary Failure*, Rutgers University Press, 1941, pp. 341-63, 406.

his former practices, he would as often as not have discarded. While
Freneau had a pencil in his hand there could be little essential final-
ity in the text of any of his poems. Therefore, in some instances when
confronted with a choice between two or more versions, I have repro-
duced that which seemed to me most certainly the one which the poet
himself would finally have approved. This, of course, was often a
matter of intuitive interpretation on my part. In order to allow other
students of Freneau the same right of interpretation, significant
verbal variations are indicated in the *Notes* at the end of the pres-
ent volume. And Freneau's titles, which are sometimes almost as
long as the poems they head, have in many instances been shortened:
the complete original title of each poem, together with changes in
subsequent printings, will also be found in the *Notes*. As an *Appendix*
I have listed additional poems which, though they cannot irrefutably
be attributed to Freneau, appeared in the same newspapers during
the same period and which seem to me very much in his manner and
idiom.

The student of American poetry will find little among the last
poems of Freneau which adds either to his knowledge of the poet or
to the poet's literary stature. Most of them simply restate themes
which Freneau had often expressed before. Others relive in retro-
spect scenes and events of the past from which he had seen his coun-
try born. A few contemplate, as Freneau had always contemplated
with enthusiastic interest, new schemes for human improvement or
new evidences of the rational perfectibility of man. Occasionally he
turned now, as he had often been quick to turn before, in satire
against those who in any way obstructed his tenacious ideal of free-
dom and happiness for all men; but the satire was more gentle now,
tempered by his years and the disappointments of his own literary
experiences. Liberal historians may notice with interest the old poet's
attitude toward the European adventures of Washington Irving and
will find in the narrative poem "Elijah" an instructive contemporary
commentary on the westward migration of New Englanders. The his-
torian of ideas may discover a challenging tangle of contradictions
in Freneau's "philosophy," but the belletristic critic will find little
to excite him. Even those of us who delight to follow, with more
sentiment perhaps than scholarship, the trials and errors of other

men who tried and often failed to get their thoughts on paper, will
pause in agreement when, reviewing his literary career, the old poet
admits

> To write was my sad destiny,
> The worst of trades, we all agree.

But even so these verses deserve better than to be buried among
yellowing files of tattered newspapers. Philip Freneau himself tried
to publish them in a volume, but the countrymen whom he had faith-
fully served for half a century were interested then in other things.
This is not the book which the poet himself would have published—
at least two poems too long for newspaper columns are missing, and
the text, in spite of most careful efforts, is undoubtedly not in just
the form he would finally have approved it. *The Last Poems of
Philip Freneau* does not pretend to be a scholarly book, not even, in
essence, a book for scholars. It is simply an effort to bring together
some of the poems which Freneau apparently wanted preserved and
to present them, to the best of sympathetic ability, in a form most
representative of them and their author. We may think of it, if we
wish, as a belated token of appreciation for what one man accom-
plished during his lifetime in defense of what we in our generation
have codified as "The Four Freedoms." These are times when we
may well be reminded of the stand made by Americans of a former
age for principles in which they believed. And when we name these
earlier Americans, each glorious in his obstinacy, in justice we may
not

> let that "veteran poet" be forgot
> Simple in tongue, but eloquent in thought,
> Who rose in ages, when the wheels of war,
> Trod letters down beneath her fiery car:
>
> . . .
>
> Let the old Bard, whose patriot voice has fann'd
> The fire of Freedom that redeem'd our land,
> Live on the scroll with kindred names that swell
> The page of history, where their honours dwell.

Duke University   LEWIS LEARY

THE LAST POEMS OF PHILIP FRENEAU

Stanzas on the Great Comet: To Ismenia

This brilliant stranger from afar,
Does he portend the storms of war:
Parading in the blue expanse,
Does he predict the doom of France?

Perhaps on nobler business sent!
He hovers o'er our continent:
These comets are prodigious things,
They fly without the aid of wings:
From whence they came, or where they go,
You cannot tell, nor do I know.

Do they, indeed, about the sun
In parabolic orbits run?—
It may be so—and some have said
This convex Earth, on which we tread,
This Earth, which now in circles roll'd
Is such an orbit mov'd of old!

Then, sailing through the etherial blue,
The mighty mass, projected, flew
And in the solar beams array'd,
A formidable tail display'd!

Who knows but, as this Comet rolls,
She comes to take a freight of souls,
The souls on earth condemned to wait
Translation to the Comet State.

The blazing Comet, now in sight,
Far southward travels day and night,
It keeps its circle round the pole
And sees the planets near it roll,
But never will their course molest
'Till the Creator sees it best.

Who knows but in yon flaming sphere
The souls from parted bodies are,
Are cloath'd again in nobler dress,
In the Comet find all happiness.

Who knows but, when she quits us here,
The mind is destined to that sphere,
May, while we *here* her husk entomb,
In Jove's celestial gardens bloom.

If near the sun this Comet strays,
His heated atmospheric rays
May bring new seasons to his clime,
No doubt, his Spring, or Summer time.

His harvests, then, are gather'd in,
His Autumn will its course begin,
When e'er its tail, to disappear,
Becomes a circumambient sphere.

When far remote, beyond our ken
Receding from the view of men,
The Comet shall his course pursue
'Till his aphelion comes in view,

Then is his winter, then his folks
Sit snug at home and pass their jokes,
No doubt, enjoy the evening fire,
The glass, the parson, and the 'squire,
See oceans rage, hear tempests blow,
And scorn them all—as we do now.

The Neglected Husband

A man's best fortune or his worst's a wife,
A steady friendship, or continual strife.
  Poor Richard, once married a Belle,
    The pride, and the toast of the town,
  He could love her, he thought, very well,
    Let her smile, let her scold, let her frown.

  She danced—and she cared not a straw,
    Not a fig, if he lived or he died;
  If a fop with a feather she saw
    His *attentions* were rarely denied.

  Poor Richard was pitied by all,
    Thus slighted, neglected, distress'd,
  Yet, rather than wrangle and brawl
    He made of his bargain the best.

  In reading, he pass'd all the day,
    Or posing the works of the dead;
  He scribbled a little, they say,
    When the notion came into his head.

  No sooner the candles were lit
    Than Richard neglected the pen—
  She cared not a cent what he writ,
    Or thought, about women or men.

  While he was intent on a book,
    She flirted away to the ball;
  And told him, he sadly mistook,
    For *cards* were the best of them all.

  At last, honest Richard fell sick,
    She saw it, and said with a groan,
  "I see you are going *my* Dick,
    And *therefore* I let you alone.

The Doctors know best what to do;
  For doses and drenches prepare;
There's Dolly, and Sambo, and Sue—
  I leave you, *my dear,* in their care."—

He fretted to see her depart
  In a humor so cheerful and gay,
And said, with a sigh from his heart,
  These women will have their own way.

Poor Richard survived but a year
  The cruel neglect of his spouse,
Yet loved her, and call'd her *his dear*—
  But thought she had broken *church vows.*

When death came at last to his aid,
  He muttered with groaning, and pain,
I am going, he peevishly said,
  Where I never will marry again.

Then gave up the ghost, with a groan,
  And sunk to the land of repose,
Where madam must go, in her turn,
  When rid of her dandies and beaus.

What follow'd, we scarcely need say,
  Nor think if I do that I rave,
She dress'd and she went to the Play,
  And Richard was laid in his grave.

Stanzas Written for a Lad

Eternal praise to thee, my God,
　Who guards me when the danger's nigh,
Preventing all my steps abroad
　From lighting on the serpent sly.

How near was I to death's cold shade,
　When the other step had been my last,
But *thou* art still my constant aid,
　Both for the present and the past.

When wandering through the desert gloom,
　No thought had I of *death so near;*
No thought, in youth's progressing bloom,
　That life was just concluding here!

Or, had thy vision so decreed,
　That his cursed head should bruise my heel;
And, for my sins, that I should bleed,
　Thy judgment had been righteous still.

The subtle poisin through each vein,
　Had then thy God-like image foiled,
And, through excess of rage and pain,
　Faint nature had in death recoiled.—

Since GOD of me hath mindful been,
　To guard me from this treacherous foe,
My endless praises he shall win
　And all the world his mercies know.

To Mr. Blanchard, the Celebrated Aeronaut

Nil Mortalibus ard unum lest
Coelum ipsum *petimus* stuttistra.

HORACE.

From Persian looms the silk *he* wove
No *Weaver* meant should trail above
The surface of the earth we tread,
To deck the matron or the maid.

But *you* ambitious, have design'd
With silk to soar above mankind:—
On silk you hang your splendid car
And mount towards the morning star.

How can you be so careless—gay:
Would you amidst red lightnings play;
Meet sulphurous blasts, and fear them not—
Is Phaeton's sad fate forgot? [1]

Beyond our view you mean to rise—
And *this Balloon,* of mighty size,
Will to the astonish'd eye appear,
An atom wafted thro' the air.

Where would you rove? amidst the storms,
Departed Ghosts, and shadowy forms,
Vast tracts of aether, and, what's more,
A sea of space without a shore!—

Would you to Herschell find the way—
To Saturn's Moons, undaunted stray;
Or, wafted on a silken wing,
Alight on Saturn's double ring?

[1] See the second Book of Ovid's Metamorphosis, for the history of Phaeton (Freneau's note).

8

Would you the lunar mountains trace,
Or in her flight fair Venus chase;
Would you, like her, perform the tour
Of sixty thousand miles an hour?—

To move at such a dreadful rate
He must propel, who did create—
By him, indeed, are wonders done
Who follows Venus round the sun.

At Mars arriv'd, what would you see!—
Strange forms, I guess—not such as we;
Alarming shapes, yet seen by none;
For every planet has its own.

If onward still, you urge your flight
You may approach some satellite,
Some of the shining train above
That circle round the orb of Jove.

Attracted by so huge a sphere
You might become a stranger here:
There you might be, if there you fly,
A giant sixty fathoms high.

May heaven preserve you from that fate!
Here, men are men of little weight:
There, Polypheme, it might be shown,
Is but a middle sized baboom.—

This ramble through, the æther pass'd,
Pray tell us when you stop at last;
Would you with gods that æther share,
Or dine on atmospheric air?—

You have a longing for the skies,
To leave the fogs that round us rise,

To haste your flight and speed your wings
Beyond this world of little things.

Your silken project is too great;
Stay here, Blanchard, 'till death or fate
To which, yourself, like us, must bow,
Shall send you where you want to go.

Yes—wait, and let the heav'ns decide;—
Your wishes may be gratified,
And you shall go, as swift as thought,
Where nature has more finely wrought,

Her Chrystal spheres, her heavens serene;
A more sublime, enchanting scene
Than thought depicts or poets feign.

The Fortunate Blacksmith

YOUNG Vulcan long had aim'd a dart
At fair Priscilla's *iron* heart,
And, after all, with much ado,
Hard work he had to pierce it through.

He swore, when he the maid caress'd,
She carried *anvils* in her breast;
"*A heavy sledge, at least,* said he,
Come hither friends, and pity me!"

What power shall melt this flinty maid;
This nymph of *steel* we should have said,
What *bellows* shall its torrent cast
To put love's furnace in a blast!

It made her blush, it hurt her pride
In *steel* or iron to confide;
To *love*, to wed a hammering lad,
The world, she guess'd, would think her mad.

He often threatened to be off,
And drown him in the *tempering trough*,
His life he purposed to destroy,
And yet the nymph continued coy.

"A man that wrought at such a trade!
I cannot bear an *iron* blade"
She wanted *Gold*, that dearer ore,
Which every nymph is hunting for.

At length, he drew a Lottery Prize!
The *iron* melted in her eyes.
The *anvil* from her breast she shoved,
And said, your suit is *now* approv'd

11

The arrow that the nymph did win
Was headed with a silver pin—
And now approach'd the wedding day;
To church the lovers took their way:

The envy, *she,* of every maid,
And *he,* an honour to his trade,
While through the streets the note resounds,
A blacksmith with a thousand pounds!

The Bride will look as black as night!
May Spanish dollars make her white,
May blacksmiths from this union rise
And not their father's trade despise.

Salutary Maxims,
Or, *the Way of the World.*
To a Misanthrope, or Man-Hater.

Would you peace and safety find,
To live in quiet with mankind,
Do not quarrel with their *notions;*
Let each have his own devotions;
Interfere not with their strife,
Take no part with man or wife;
Meddle not with *satire's* pen,
Make no friendship with *mean men;*
Blow not up foul discord's bellows,
Drink no liquor with rude fellows;
Fools, at best that gape and grin,
Devils, when the liquor's in.
More than all, I would advise
Always act with *some disguise:*
Strive to do not too much good—
Let these rules be understood,
With *another* we would mention
That would hinder much dissention,
Scolding hags and peevish men,
Shun them as a lion's den;
Hug and kiss the girl you love,
But hope no angels from above.
Dream not of *celestial charms;*
You clasp no goddess in your arms—
Goddesses are sometimes made—
Quite enough, to spoil the trade.
To *command* the pure good will
Of human kind, remember, still,
This is the SECRET, *this is the charm*—
DO THEM NEITHER—GOOD NOR HARM.

Stanzas Written in an Ancient Burial Ground

"When troubles come, and cares perplex,
  (An ancient Roman said)
"We have the right, and tis the best
To mingle with the dead"

This we deny—when cares distract,
  And days of woe arrive;
'Tis wrong to do the coward act,
  'Tis nobler, far, to *live*.

These, discontented with the cheerful day,
Tired of a Sun that gave them no delight.
With life disgust'ed, forced their grovelling way,
To the dark chambers of eternal night.

If from the skies a spark celestial came
That warms our clay, a spirit that commands,
For some wise cause, it animates our frame,
Here doom'd to stay 'till fate dissolves the bands.

Who'er thou art that with presumptive hand
Aims at the heart the death conducting steel,
Not guiltless at the awful Bar will stand,
Were all are judged, and doom'd without appeal.

Life is probation—all our years a task,
A task of toil—but with it man should bear,
'Till life's rude winter, and its storms, are past
And brighter scenes in brighter worlds appear.

Epitaph Upon a Spanish Horse

HERE rest the bones of ROYAL GIFT
Safe interr'd at *Dead man's Lift;*
Now no longer strong or swift.

As my pen is rather weak
May I, sirs, your pardon seek,
If the horse himself shall speak:

"Favourite of our King of Spain,
Oft he held my tightening rein,
Briskly cantering o'er the plain.

"Round the Prado, at Madrid
Many a time the monarch rid
With strange fancies in his head,

"One of which I will disclose,
Safely *now,* I may suppose:—
Hear it then, my friends and foes.

"Travelling on a plashy road
With my ever honored load
I threw my master in the mud.

"*This* was more than once repeated
Till the king got overheated,
On my back no more he seated.

"Angry at my vicious way,
He sent me to America
To witness presidential sway.

"He sent me here, without Petition,
T' escape the Holy Inquisition;
Such the purpose of my mission.

"Weary of the *Royal Plan,*
Hither I came to find a man,
And die—a GOOD REPUBLICAN."

15

The Tye-Wig

THOUGH now you *seem* to look so gay,
I think I hear the Tye-Wig say,
"You might have worn *me* in your youth,
Or even a Tye-Wig more uncouth,
When blood ran brisk, and Fancy said
JACOB! assist the barber's trade."—

This foppish wig will not recall
The days of youth, your vernal prime,
When months and years were cheery, all,
And *Nature,* in her summer time,
Thus sung to all who chose to hear,
My Summer lasts not all the year.

As summer gives to Autumn place,
As *fair* succeeds to *rain,*
So we retire—another race
Comes laughing o'er the plain:
Well!—let them jest, and laugh and play:
We had our turn, and so have they.

Such wigs, with pleasure, some might view
When *five and twenty* was in bloom;
But what are wigs, like this, to you,
Now lingering near the silent tomb?—
Such wigs become not *sixty eight,*
Grey hairs would better suit your pate.

It hides no wrinkles in your face,
Your tottering step it can't conceal;
In every step old age we trace,
That sees you travelling down the hill:—
Then throw this boyish wig away
And wear again your head of grey.

Letitia

Young girls have their *notions*, we see every day,
    And notions, why should they have not?
The world is but notions, Philosophers say,
    And whims are humanity's lot.

A girl had a *notion* to love a young man,
    And, who was the youngster—? (say you)
He was a young blacksmith, for tell it I can,
    But his *name* shall be kept out of view.

Yet the heart of the Blacksmith, as hard as a rock,
    Refus'd to return her regard—
His door of affection he would not unlock,
    Which the nymph took abundantly hard.

She vow'd that she lov'd him, and said with a squeal,
    How blest might we travel thro' life,
Yourself at your anvil and I at my wheel,
    The fondest and faithfullest wife!

But still he refused to comply with her wish,
    And told her he did not admire—
Go, look somewhere else, he said, Madam *Fish*,
    Some lover to warm with your fire.

She griev'd and she groan'd, and had like to have died;
    Some thought she would quickly depart:
But still she had left, in her bosom, some pride,
    And slighted Letitia took heart.

With the earnings—not much—at her wheel she had made,
    With dollars that long had laid by,
She bought her a ticket and angrily said,
    My fortune, I vow, I will try!—

And Fortune, for once, was propitious and kind—
  This spinster so humble and poor,
Drew a prize—and a prize that was much to her mind—
  Some thousands, at least, we are sure.

The prize it was such as a king would be proud
  To receive—or a Princess implore—
It enabled *Letitia* (et ceteras allowed)
  To ride in a chariot and four!

The Blacksmith aghast!—heard the news, with a groan,
  But went cap-in-hand to her door:
He met her, and said, I have come to atone,
  For the love that I slighted before.

I lov'd you too well!—I was only in jest
  When I told you *I could not admire;*
I only was waiting to be the more blest
  When the days of my service expire.—

She answered—your usage I now will repay;
  When I lov'd you, why did you love not?
Your hand should have join'd to my hand on that day,
  Should have struck when the iron was hot!

A Dialogue
Between a News-Printer
And His Cash-Collector

PRINTER.—Well, sir, and what have you brought me to-day?

COLLECTOR.—I have brought you *myself*—and that's all I've to say.

P.—No money, no dollars in specie nor notes

C.—Not a sixpence, a shilling, to moisten our throats.

P.—Bless me!—and how do they think that we live?

C.—They think not of that while the news you will *give*.

P.—Did they make no excuses—no promise to pay?

C.—Some tell me to call next April or May.

P.—Next April or May!—we shall starve before then,
 The devil, I think, has got into some men.
 Next April or May!—my subscribers are mad—
 Go dun them again, and say, cash must be had!

C.—Go dun them again!—I have dunn'd till 'm sick;
 Six months for my board, I have run upon tick,—
 My landlord has growl'd, that I pay not a cent,
 And swears I must pay, or he can't pay his rent.

P.—They have dollars, by dozens, to go to the play,
 At balls and assemblies *some* shine very gay,
 But, *pay your subscription!*—they have not a shilling!

C.—They have it, I guess, but to pay are unwilling.

P.—Since the day that old Noah came out of his ark,
 I am sorry to say, but am forced to remark,
 For some mischief committed, some crime, or some sin,
 There ne'er were such times as the times we are in.
 The maker of paper has dunn'd me—so, so,—
 And his money must have, or to jail I must go.

C.—The maker of paper!—the landlord is nigh,
 And a bailiff attends him—you'll see by and by.

P.—A Bailiff!—'odzooks, it is time to take care,
 As soon would I meet with a wolf or a bear.

C.—If they do not pay you, you cannot pay me,
 Next winter is coming, and sir, do ye see,

19

Unless pretty shortly our landlords we pay
I strongly suspect we must both run away.
P.—I hope not so bad—but before that we run,
Accost them again, with a positive dun,
Be modest and mild when you ask for our dues,
But tell them, *no pay, and we give you no news.*

The Great Western Canal

Meliusne sylvas ire per longas
Fuit, an recentes carpere undas?
            —HORACE.

i.e. which was best—to travel through tedious, dreary forests, or
to sail on these recent waters?

The nation true to honor's cause,
To *equal rights* and *equal laws*,
Is well secured, and well released
From the proud monarchs of the east.

Thus *Holland* rose from *Spain's* control,
And thus shall rise from pole to pole
Those systems formed on reason's plan
That vindicate the *Rights of man.*—

Nature, herself, will change her face,
And arts fond arms the world embrace;
In works of peace mankind engage,
And close the despot's iron age.

And *here* behold a work progress,
Advancing through the wilderness,
A work, so recently began,
Where Liberty enlightens man:
Her powerful voice, at length, awakes
Imprisoned seas and bounded lakes.

The great idea to pursue,
To *lead the veins the system through;*
Such glorious toils to emulate,
Should be the task of every *State.*

From *Erie's* shores to *Hudson's* stream
The unrivalled work would endless seem;
Would *millions* for the work demand,
And half depopulate the land.

To *Fancy's* view, what years must run,
What ages, till the task is done!
Even *truth,* severe would seem to say,
One hundred years must pass away:—

The sons might see what sires began,
Still unperformed the mighty plan,
The impeded barque, in durance held,
By hills confined, by rocks repelled.—

Not *China's* wall, though grand and strong,
Five hundred leagues it towers along,
No China's wall, though stretching far,
With this vast object can compare,

With such gigantic works of old
This proud *Canal* may be enrolled,
Which to our use no tyrant gave
Nor owes its grandeur to one Slave.—

If kings their object tribes compell'd
With toil immense, such walls to build,
A *new Republic* in the west
(A great example to the rest)
Can seas unite, and *here* will shew
What Freedom's nervous sons can do.

See Commerce *here* expand her sail,
And distant shores those waters hail,
As wafting to Manhattan's coast
The products that new regions boast.

And hence our fleets transport their freights
To jealous kings and sister states,
And spread her fame from shore to shore,
Where suns ascend, or billows roar,

To make the purpose all complete,
Before they bid *two oceans* meet,
Before the task is finished all,
What rocks must yield, what forests fall?

Three years elapsed, behold it done!
A work from Nature's *chaos* won;
By hearts of oak and hands of toil
The Spade inverts the rugged soil
A work, that may remain secure
While suns exist and Moons endure.

With patient step I see them move
O'er many a plain, through many a grove;
Herculean strength disdains the sod
Where tigers ranged or *Mohawks* trod;
The powers that can the soil subdue
Will see the mighty project through.

Ye patrons of this bold design
Who *Erie* to the *Atlantic* join,
To you be every honour paid—
No time shall see your fame decayed:—
Through gloomy groves you traced the plan,
The rude abodes of savage man.

Ye Prompters of a work so vast
That may for years, for centuries last;
Where Nature toiled to bar the way
You mark'd her steps, but changed her sway.

Ye Artists, who, with skillful hand,
Conduct such rivers through the land,
Proceed!—and in your bold career
May every Plan as wise appear,
As *this*, which joins to *Hudson's* wave
What Nature to *St. Lawrence* gave.

The Re-opening of the Park Theatre

Though lost awhile to *this*, the Muses' seat,
Once more, kind patrons, here once more we meet:
To wasting flames you saw this dome consigned
Where Reason's feast gave pleasure to the mind.
If wasting flames deprived you of the PLAY,
This night restores what Fortune snatched away,
Improved in all the Drama's votaries prize
Nor rigid reason would, itself, despise.

Be it your's no longer to regret the past,
And our's to find amusement to your taste;
Our's is the hope to merit all you give,
And gain your favor, as by *you* we live;
Our's be the task, unmoved by smiles or spleen,
To grace each act, and live through every scene.

What changes pass on Time's unsettled stage,
Events how various mark each following age!
Perhaps *this spot*, where *Thespis* takes her stand,
Once held a *wigwam* in a savage land;
Its surly chief an angry visage bore,
And war and slaughter stained his path with gore;
His boiling veins with poisonous rancor swelled,
Or, where compassion touched, the hand rebelled.

Here, once, perhaps, with dart or bended bow,
The savage prowled three centuries ago,
Where painted tribes their swarthy mates possessed,
With love's fine flame a stranger to the breast—
Here strolled the native, and his hideous squaw,
And ruled the female with despotic law;—
No right she claimed that guardian Nature gave,
By tyrant custom dwindled to a slave.

Such was their doom!—To chace the timorous deer,
Dislodge the *Elk* or circumvient the *Bear*
Belonged to *Men*—to craft and warfare bred,
Through gloomy groves their vagrant tribes they led,
Ere HUDSON'S Galley passed *Manhattan's* isle,[1]
Or *England's* sceptre swayed the *Indian* soil.

Behold the change! where grew the shaded wild,
And simple Nature, solitary, smiled,
New social manners, peace, and commerce reign,
And pleasures meet, with plenty in their train;
Now spires ascend, and splendid streets appear,
And beauty, female beauty, charms us here;
With every art that human skill designed
To grace the person or exalt the mind.

To pass the amusing hours, that all desire,
New *Plays*, new *subjects*, justly you require;
For *these*, on *Europe*, still our Stage relies,
And *Europe*, *Europe* every want supplies,
Why sleeps COLUMBIA'S genius for the stage—
Can not one *Bard* arise, to glad the age,
Not one be found to abandon flimsey rhymes,
And rise the *Shakespeare* of our modern times?

'Tis from the Stage in every land we trace
A polished people or a barbarous race
With Greece enslaved the *Thespian* spirit failed,
And *Rome's* great *Drama* fell when *Goths* prevailed.[2]

[1] Early in September, 1609—Some say 1608.

[2] Ancient Rome had many vast amphitheatres and circuses.—These were, for the most part, demolished or dismantled by an immense army of Barbarians, under *Alaric*, the Gothic General, about the year of Christ 850. One of these was still standing, at least the walls, about a century ago, or which *Addison* says,

> "An Amphitheatre's amazing height
> Here strikes the eye with wonder and delight;
> Which, on its public days, unpeopled Rome,
> And held uncrowded nations in its womb."

No more the scene a crowded audience drew,
The wild barbarian spurned the splendid SHEW!
No more the tragic Muse bade nations weep,
No more the comic act lulled care to sleep;
No living scene displayed the painter's art,
No music, with its chorus, thrilled the heart;
No long oblivion seized the enfeebled mind,
And, as the Nation sunk, the Stage declined!

Ye friends and patrons of the *Thespian* Muse,
Our failings pardon, and our faults excuse,
Still to improve, shall be our dearest aim,
Since full perfection few may dare to claim—
Arise, young Authors, on COLUMBIA'S soil,
And give us SOMETHING NEW, to cheer our toil,
Thus shall the Muse reanimate the Stage,
And more than *Shakespeare* glow through every page!

Jersey City

On this black height is seen a wide display
Of rivers, towns and mountains far away;
A city vast and splendid to the view,
Another *London,* with its follies too.

London, Britannia's pride, that powerful isle,
The land of heroes, that prolific soil,
Where half its harvests from its *filth* have sprung,
And half its soil is formed of *men they hung;*
—*London,* whose commerce through the world extends,
London, who ship-loads of her NOVELS sends;
London, sweet town, where scribbling is a trade.
From the vain Countess to her chamber-maid;
London, a tyrant in the times by-past,
Will fix our manners and our fate at last.

While *here* I pause or make some brief delay,
Why should I cancel what I mean to say?
Amidst these tombs I pen my cheerless strain,
A *City,* rising on the adjacent plain;
Demands a sigh!—in truth, so slow to rise,
To rival YORK would ask ten centuries.

Howe'er that be, while *here* I take my stand
Between *two rivers* that confine the land,
In one short hour before I migrate hence,
I write my thoughts, I hope without offence;
I treat the church, the tombs, with due respect,
The priest is absent, and I write unchecked.

If some are wrath, and deem me too severe,
They must indulge their wrath, the case is clear;
One truth stands firm, till truth itself shall cease,
All nature's discord makes all nature's peace.

All here is nature, beauty, some have said,
Whether you court the sun, or woo the shade.
Near yon thronged inn the market-folks we see,
Patterns of perfect beauty all agree;
Whether the flush of blooming beauty glows
On *Margery's* cheek or *Knickerbocker's* nose,
Still all is *beauty,* in a hundred ways,
Respect demanding, or commanding praise—
For *Plato* wrote, and *Tully* did opine,
Nature is handsome when not quite divine.

Dear infant city!—how can you but fall,
When proud *Manhattan* claims the *Hudson,* all?
Where Neptune drives his billows to your strand,
So far her charters and her claims extend.

Her's were your prospect, but not her's your fate,
To rise, unrivalled, in commercial weight.
This jealous sister dreads the approaching sail,
Your square-rigg'd vessels, and becalms the gale.
With selfish eye her sons of trade—and LUCK
Claim *Holdfast* for their favourite dog—my duck; [1]
Look when they will to *Jersey,* and her town,
The hourly watch-word stuns me—KEEP HER DOWN.

To these old tombs once more I turn my view;
Here slumber *some,* who once were *selfish* too,
Here slumber some, whose God was wealth and gold,
Who grasped at worlds, and planets would have sold,
Whose livers swelled to see a neighbor thrive,
And to another's welfare scarce alive.

Where are they now! and where the wealth they prized?
All scattered, vanished, spent, monopolized;

[1] . . . "Trust none, trust none!
Men's oaths are wafer-cakes, mere sullabie,
And Holdfast is the only dog, my duck."

To thankless heirs, perhaps, has found its way,
To heirs as selfish, and as base as they.

Learn hence, ye envious, to retract your plans,
And be content with just, but equal gains.
The *Hudson* should for JERSEY CITY flow,
And aid her commerce, as it prospered you.

The City Poet

Let such on custards and fine cakes be fed
And we, plain country Bards, eat barley bread.

You court the favours of the town,
You carry verses up and down,
    You scribble for the stage—
Who would pursue so poor a trade,
Such *debts of honor,* badly paid
    For many a labored prize?

To steer a boat, or drive a cart,
To practice some mechanic art,
    Yields something for your pain;
But poems are in no demand,
Few read them, fewer understand
    The visions of your brain.

Let Poets choose some gainful trade,
And not depend on Clio's aid—
    With all the muse's skill,
With all the drama in his scull
Shakespeare was bred *to combing wool,*
    And *Plautus* turned a mill.

Of all the Poets dead and gone,
I cannot recollect but ONE
    That throve by writing rhyme—
If *Pope* from *Homer* gained rewards,
Remember, statesmen, kings and lords
    Were poets, in his time.

A poet where there is no king,
Is but a disregarded thing

31

An atom on the wheel;
A second *Iliad* could he write
His pockets would be very light,
And beggarly his meal.

The SHERIFF *only* deals in prose,
And *prisons* have a hundred woes;—
With *debts*, you have no *dues*—
You have no thousands in the Bank,
You float upon a rotten plank—
—Go home, and mend your shoes.

Elijah,
The New England Emigrant.
No. I

The wedded pair began to look
Askance, on father's chimney smoke;
And many a scheme is set afloat
To quit the old paternal spot,
And seek, in places little known,
Both smoke, and smoke-house of their own.

Around the field, with rueful eye,
A yankee walked, and many a sigh—
A yankee of an ancient stock,
The pilgrims of the *Plymouth Rock;*
Then, casting one fond glance on SUE,
He said, "My dear—it will not do!

"This field, this soil, so old and worn,
Has seen two hundred crops of corn:
Here *onions* throve in seasons past,
But *onions* will not always last;
Here, *barley* grew some years ago,
But barley will not always grow.
At least, it grows so poor and lean
I am ashamed it should be seen;
I did my best to make manure
But blights and blasts have made us poor."
Susannah answered, with a tear,
"Then what, *Ei-jah*, do we here?

"For all I sewed or all I spun,
I have to send the hourly *dun;*
Of all my *truck*, in yonder dell,
Three *pumpkins* only prospered well;

The crop is perished in the ground,
That might have brought me—twenty pound,
Of all my dear potatoe patch,
There never yet was seen the match,
When, yesterday, amidst the dew,
To boil with pork, I scratched a few,
A boy that came from *Nabby's* hut,
Mistook them for the hickory nut.
The matter is as clear as glass
That we must join the beggar class.—
On household stuff that *man of law*,
The *Sheriff*, soon will have his paw.
I dread to see provision scant,
The oven cold—the house in want."

ELIJAH

Before that you shall want, my duck,
I'll grub the bog, or fall the oak,
Make forests bow, where'er they grow,
And rivers wait, where'er they flow—
In boat, or cart, I take my *trick*,
And fight the *Red-Men*—with my stick.

If once resolved to emigrate
We soon may reach another state.
Of climates we can take our choice—
What say you to the *Illinois?*
That country felt not *Adam's* course,
If we may credit Doctor *Morse*,
Who styles it Plenty's favorite seat,
And paints a paradise complete.
By all that's good, this white-oak chest
May reach *Missouri* in the west:
Shall travel hard, thro' thick and thin,
With double lock on what's therein,

The chest that holds, safe folded down,
Among the rest, your wedding gown.

These oxen, comrades of my toil,
May yet, on *Alabama's* soil,
In pastures feed, and fields explore,
Such as they never knew before.
I'll pitch my tent, and boil my pot,
Where folks may purchase, steal, or SQUAT.

While light of heart, tho' scant of cash,
No doubt have I to see *Wabash;*
Adown the *Mississippi* stream,
I'll travel by the power of *steam;*—
And thus we sail, my Susan dear,
From *Baton Rouge* to *Bayou Pierre*—
We go, where plenty decks the plains,
And Summer suns rear sugar canes.

To such blest scenes of joy complete
Will you and I, dear girl, retreat,
Where Nature, with a liberal hand,
Displays abundance through the land;
And not, as where by frosts oppressed,
We squeeze—a nothing—from her breast.

SUSANNAH

Elijah, were we each divorced,
And things were at the very worst,
Should deacon *Nathan* press his suit,
Or *Congress men,* of more repute;
Had they ten thousands in the Bank,
And moving in the foremost rank—
Were you as crooked as a bow,
Or hump-backed as a buffaloe,
As poor as *Job* (and all agree

That none could be more poor than he)
I would reject their suit, with scorn,
And journey with you to *Cape Horne.*

ELIJAH

Were you as homely as a squaw,
And wore a bonnet, made of straw,
Still for the virtues of the mind,
Such *Spirit,* with *discretion* joined;
Were I a single man again
I would be headmost in your train;
I would prefer a lass, like you,
To all that *princes* ever knew—
God help us, if you had a nose
As long as what I might suppose,
Still I would swear from *mental* charms,
I clasped a Goddess in my arms.

But ere we bid our last adieu,
We must consult your father, too;—
To keep ourselves, and *bantling,* warm,
We rent a corner of his farm.
He once paraded to the west,
And home, again, he came distressed;—
We must discourse him on our plan,
So, off—and see the good old man.

Elijah,
The New England Emigrant.
No. II

A Deacon of a church hard by
Was Susan's father, rough and dry,
Advanced in years, and somewhat deaf
To which a trumpet gave relief.
This father lived a few miles back,
And not remote from Merrimack; [1]
He had a deal of inward light,
With both his chimnies painted white,
And oftentimes his head he shook
At people of a lousy look,
And often made this shrewd remark,
A shabby pilot steers the barque.
And to his name was tacked ESQUIRE,
A *title* common folks admire.
As one that joined him to the *elect,*
And one that made him *circumspect.*—
His name was HEZEKIAH SALEM,
Whose heart and hand did never fail him,
Except, when, once, a whooping pack
Of *Choctaw* Indians drove him back:
And nearly had his head trepann'd
For settling on unpurchased land—
To him she goes to ask advice,
Gets—and forgets it in a trice.

SUSANNAH

Well, Father, I am on the wing
To say—a—very—serious—thing.
Elijah is quite discontented
With this same lot from you he rented.
He wants to go to *Batten-Rugs.* [2]

[1] A considerable river in the eastern part of Massachusetts.
[2] Baton Rouge, a military post on the Mississippi.

Since here in vain he toils and tugs.
The road is long—how will it do?
And yet I *dread* [3] to part with *you,*
Who always were so kind and good,
Supplied me cloathes, provided food.

HEZEKIAH

Speak louder, Girl—it seems to me,
Your voice has lost its usual key.

SUSANNAH

I say, in brief, we talk of late,
And have some thoughts to emigrate,
Where things will wear a better face,
To Batten-Rugs—or some such place!

HEZEKIAH

To Batten-Rugs?—and where is that?
A place I never heard of yet—
You think to go to Batten-Rugs,
No doubt, to breed and fatten hogs . . .
It is a distant place, I think,
And near the *Mississippi* brink:—
Two thousand miles make *far away;*
No, Susan, Susan, you must stay.
Elijah must be, surely, mad,
To take such notions in his head.
But, did you know the *Indian race,*
The people of the wilderness,
The tribes that yet possess the west,
The people of a flinty breast,
With hearts as hard as granite rock,
With sculls as thick as barber's block;
You would remain contented here
Where few or none can give us fear.

[3] I grieve.

A race they are, with teeth like knives,
With whom in vain the *Spirit* strives;
A race, whose hands are armed with claws,
And scythes are planted in their jaws.

No! I advise you to remain
Here, steady to your native plain.
Remember what the *quakers* say,
(Whose maxims often come in play,)
That evil to the couple clings
Who slight the day of little things.
And in your brains this proverb toss,
A rolling stone collects no moss.
A farm on *Alabama's* streams
Might do in JOEL BARLOW's dreams . . .
Such rhyming dealers in romance
See Nature only in a trance.—
If you embrace Elijah's whim,
Your future fortune is with HIM—
So, rather than come snivelling back
You'd better stay at *Merrimack*—
If you on airy nothings fix,
Still, I'm no fool at sixty-six.

SUSANNAH

O Father! how can you reflect
On JOEL, whom I so respect.
How can you thus decry the page
Of the first poet of the age?
He is an author I admire,
In reading whom I never tire . . .
Recall your words—at least explain—
For I must say, and will maintain
That he, who would surpass that bard,
Must travel far, and study hard;
Must view mankind in court and camp,
And often trim the midnight lamp,

To bring, in so sublime a strain,
Columbus on the stage again.[4]

But to go on as we began,
Elijah is no *common man;*
He is, at least, six feet of length,
And gifted with *Goliah's* strength.
Elijah says, the savage pack
Will never make him turn his back.
And, armed with staff of seasoned oak,
No mortal can endure his stroke;
Nor will the boldest chief presume
To seize one feather from his plume
Then what has such a man to fear
From such a herd as Indians are?
In boxing he is dreaded more
Than ever boxer was before;
What prowess can that force resist
Where Death resides on either fist;
Whose powerful clench, if aimed with skill,
Might leave a mark on *Bunker's Hill.*

HEZEKIAH

He fight the Indians with his stick!
The Indians soon would make him sick.
The Girl is crazed—one Indian yell
Would be to him a funeral bell.
The warrior whoop would stun his ear
And close at once his mad career.
No Susan, Susan you must stay:
Consider, I am old and gray;
Your mother is an ancient dame,
Your aunts, and uncles, much the same,
So, better here partake our rest
Than seek adventures in the west.

4 Alluding to the *Columbiad*, a Poem, by the late J. Barlow.

SUSANNAH

The BOOK in which we all believe
Bids woman *to her husband cleave.*
There is besides, another *text,*
To which a blessing is annexed—
It is a *text* that none deny,
It is—*increase and multiply.*
But, while we *here* increase our breed,
I fear they will be poor indeed,
And you would fret, and I should frown,
To see them *paupers* on the town.

HEZEKIAH

The Moon has surely cracked your brain,
That you discourse in *such a strain.*
Who taught you, hussey, thus to rave?
How many do you mean to have?
You only have *Jerusha* yet
And he will soon his living get.
But should a dozen to you fall
Still Providence would care for all.

SUSANNAH

To place our hopes on Providence
Is surely right, in common sense;
But, for provision on our shelves
We must depend upon ourselves.

HEZEKIAH

Enough!—I lay my strict command
That here you stay and work our land;
Elijah is in no condition
To undertake this crazy mission.
The time must come—is on its way—
When *you* and *he* will both be grey,

When every hour will bring its care
And Love be but a dull affair.—
Against that hour you may provide
Without this rambling, far and wide.
Then take advice, remain at home,
Nor scheme too much for days to come.
They may be good—they may be bad—
Be you but faithful to your lad,
Industrious, prudent, frugal, neat,
And all your fortune is complete!

Deep sunk these words in Susan's ears,
Who answered only with her tears;
She tucked her hair behind her comb,
And, sighing, went dejected home.

Elijah,
The New England Emigrant.
No. III

What SALEM *said Susannah tells—*
Elijah frets, and bites his nails—
They both resolve to quit the LOT
Should Salem judge it right or not.
They both agree, and think it best
To try their fortunes in the west;
But, yet, to keep their scheme concealed
'Till they could safely quit the field,
And leave a soil which barely fed,
Or, half the year denied them bread,
And which, when youth and strength were past,
Would leave them mendicants at last.

And what said Father to our notion?
(Elijah said, with some emotion;)
What thinks he of our views, and plan?
Did it not please the old gentleman?

SUSANNAH

Elijah sit you down, my dear—
Our project did not please his ear:
He said, we only dozed and dreamt,
And treated us with marked contempt,
Our journey is discouraged, all
Our purpose huddled to the wall;
It does not to his liking seem,
He thinks us crazy in the extreme—
He says the Indians will destroy us,
And *bears* and *buffaloes* annoy us,
And evils of a hundred kinds
Distract our brains, distress our minds.
Some other plan we must contrive—
In years you are but twenty-five;

And I am young, robust and hale,
Can travel over hill and dale.
Thus He, who toiled on *Laban's* land,
Took sprightly Rachel by the hand,
And, while the old dotard snored in bed,
With the fair *Syrian* damsel fled.

My mother, long ago, was placed
With those from Nature's list erased,
Where sighs and tears will nought avail 'em,
Nor cares for *Susan* or for *Salem*.
For her advice I would be glad;
But since it cannot, now, be had,
Perhaps the better part would be
With father's counsels to agree;
To live a little scant and bare,
And stay, contented, where we are.

ELIJAH

I stay, contented, where I am!!!
Give such advice to others, Ma'am.
Let father *Salem* boil his pot,
I'm careless if it boils or not;
He long has throve, and yet may rise
By ways and means that I despise;
Has made his way by *hook* and *crook*,
Nor his *own interest* once mistook,
But waddled on, through thick and thin,
Where'er he could a bargain win,
By turn and twist, through *suits* and *scandal*,
And selling trash by inch of candle—
Let him progress in such a trade—
I was for *other uses* made.
But fear, with timorous Fancy joined,
Will find a storm in every wind,
Will turn, with more than magic power,
A school-boy's wind-mill to a tower;

Will give an ape a giant's size,
Bid mole-hills into mountains rise,
And, still opposed to Reason's laws,
To masts and yards change sticks and straws.
    If *Salem* is of such a stamp,
We must desert him, and decamp.
    Young *Jehu* rigged a travelling cart,
Then, trembling asked his baby heart,
If *Indians* were not in his way,
And where they live, and where they stray?
He faultered, and was faint, do ye see,
So, ere he reached the *Chickapee* [1]
Was so discouraged, so appalled,
That his good purpose he recalled,
Returned his fortune to bewail,
And starve and die in Boston jail.
    I am not of such a feeble *make*,
Nor will I shrink when all's at stake,
Nor meanly to our hut return
At which a man of *spunk* would spurn.

SUSANNAH

    Two oxen we can call our own:
How long—to you is better known—
These oxen are not counted mean,
Not very plump, nor very lean;
We have a cart—and *there* it stands,
Made by your own ingenious hands;
There is a mare, not very old.
That, months ago, has safely foaled;
With *these* we may set out to-morrow,
And leave this land of toil and sorrow,
Where one, to thrive, must cheat and juggle,
And life is one continual struggle.
I am *impatient* to be gone—
Pray let it be to-morrow's dawn.

[1] A small river, falling into Connecticut river on the east side, at Springfield.

ELIJAH

Remember, *man* was born to *bear*,
And *woman*, too, must have her share;
(Dear Susan, do not blush and smile,
I'm talking in a decent style.)
Remember *Job*, the man of Uz,
When sick, and in a constant buzz,
The gale came on that smote his roof,
And put his *patience* to the proof
(About that period of his life,
The time he quarrelled with his wife,)
When all his household was in tears
And rafters whistling round his ears,
When beams and shingles flew, like hail,
His goods, perhaps, at sheriff's sale;
When all his *bairns* were gone to pot;
False friends—old Satan—and what not?
By his example, be resigned,
And learn serenity of mind.
Of all the virtues you have nursed,
Believe me, *Patience is the first;*
So, leave me, without further clatter,
The whole conducting of the matter.

SUSANNAH

Elijah, I am all submission,
But go with you on this condition;
I'll sit where'er we pitch our tent,
Like *Patience* on a monument,
If you will hear, like other men,
A woman's counsel now and then.
If you to western woods depart
I'll follow on, with all my heart;
The love I bear to *Yankee* land
I will forget, at your command,

Will lay my female fears aside,
And roam the forest, far and wide,
For tracts that will repay our care,
And pumpkins, to perfection, bear.
Let me enjoy some favorite whim,
And I'll attend you—sink or swim.

ELIJAH

If we but reach the western woods,
Sanduskie's hills, *Sanduskie's* floods,
My axe shall find employment there
'Till to the sun the fields lie bare,
'Till from the soil such harvests rise
As never yet have met your eyes;
Such harvests from the earth shall grow
As *Massachusetts* never knew.
For such a jaunt with me prepare,
Nor heed the weather, foul or fair,
I have of money, such a store,
As will *ten acres* buy, or more,
And, if of more to be possessed,
Let art and cunning get the rest—
Of youth and vigor, such a stock,
As may at toil and hardship mock.
A cabin I can build, and fence
My little farm at small expence;
We *Yankees* have an *active mind*,
And *all things* are to *all mankind;*
We are for all conditions made,
Contented with the *sun* or *shade*,
There you might be supremely blest,
With more than one poor *white-oak chest;*
And I, as blest as man could wish,
With twice-a-day the venison dish,
Did I possess, on acres ten,
But two domestics—COCK and HEN.

Elijah,
The New England Emigrant.
No. IV

Now, all things hid from observation,
Went on in silent preparation,
And all advanced, with caution due,
Concealed from *Salem's* wizzard view.
A woman's wits are always bright
When something future is in sight.
Susannah managed so the matter,
Elijah, with a grin, looked at her,
And said—"My dear, my dearest heart,
You act, by far, the slyest part;
We owe to *Salem* five years' rent,
With interest due at ten per cent.
To pay him off must be my care,
Or I shall be, the Lord knows where."

Susannah answered, "Never mind,
We'll leave him and his rent behind."

Both managed so their future mission
That nothing gave the least suspicion,
Both seemed contented with their lot
Though toiling hard for little got.
Susannah kept her wheel in motion,
And went to church with due devotion,
Smiling, she ate the scanty meal,
And ply'd the eternal spinning wheel,
Which, like the globe, from west to east
Revolved, and never was at rest,
Which made Susannah's fingers red,
Chafed by the furrows of the thread,
And little got for all her labor
From cousin, father, friend or neighbor.

One morning *Salem* hove in view,
And kindly asked them, "How do ye do?"

SUSANNAH

O Father!—well as well can be!

SALEM

The case is just the same with me.
But times are hard, and money scarce,
I say it, both in prose and verse,
Could sing it too, upon a pinch,
But—have you money—tell me, wench.

SUSANNAH

La! Money! Father!—not a cent,
For faster than received it went.
I sold some stockings at the stall,
But *little wants* consumed it all.

SALEM

And have you laid aside the notion
Of travelling to the *western ocean?*
Elijah!—did you count the expense?
I thought you, once, a man of sense,
But, if with purse and means so slim,
You persevere in such a whim,
I own 'tis past my comprehension
Your brains should harbor the intention.
I tell you plainly, first and last,
My thoughts are of a different cast,
Debts, due for rent, are serious things,
Landlords have eyes—and you have wings.
People are mad, to ramble far,
Better be steady where you are.
There's neighbor Isaac, and young Joe—
And they would to Kentucky go!

But, in the course of one short moon,
Came back, and sang a different tune.
Some people love to rove and wander
'Till things compel them to *knock under*.
Some aim to rove the wide world through,
And fix at last at—*Tombuctoo*.[1]

ELIJAH

We had a *notion* much the same,
(We all at *Independence* aim)
But second thoughts put all to rest,
And second thoughts are often best.
Yet, I must own, while worrying *here*,
And crawling on from year to year,
Of all we owe you for your *rent*
We cannot pay a single cent.
And therefore, in my humble view,
Some other plan might better do:
And I must honestly confess
I had rather live in the wilderness,
Than thus be dunned, and plagued, and teazed,
And even by friends and cousins squeezed;
And I must say, and you must see
The dogs are happier, far, than we.
Happy the man whose grass who tills,
And drinks at the Sanduskie hills—[2]
Recall the tune you used to play,
Over the hills, and far away!

SALEM

Drink those who will, or those who can—
I would not be that *happy man*.

[1] A large negro city on the river Niger, in the central part of Africa.
[2] A Tract of Country on the south side of Lake Erie. A new tavern erected on Sanduskie Bay.

ELIJAH

Let each his favorite plan pursue—
Neither would I, if I was you—
On Fortune's wheel you have advanced,
To every tune of Fortune danced,
Still in pursuit of *wealth* and *heaven*,
Ready to drive, or to be driven
But must confess with tears, at last,
They drove too slow or drove too fast.
And who would trust in *such a man*,
Who gains by scheming, all he can.
What farmer would confide his stock
Or cattle to *Boon Island* [3] rock,
Where all that grows is poor indeed,
For all it yields is ocean weed.
On those who quarrel with a straw
You take the vengeance of the law,
On those who, to dispel the spleen,
On Sabbath eve sing, *bonny Jean,*
You oft impose a heavy fine,
Or take them in the pillory whine;
For heedless youth you lie in wait,
Blue devils from *blue laws* create,
And all for what?—the love of gain,
Of wealth, that may not long remain.

SALEM

You lecture in a serious style—
Yet, I am *patience*, all the while,
'Tis true—it cannot be denied,
Satan is on the safer side.

ELIJAH

Could I but find contentment here,
My toils repaid each closing year,

[3] An Insular Rock, about 500 yards in length, about 4 leagues east of Portland, in he new state of Maine.

Could we but bring the year about,
And half our living mere *sour-krout*,
Not love of wealth, or love of fame,
Nor all the *Loves* that you might name,
Not SPEECHES, famed from shore to shore,
Of Congress men on Congress floor,
Not all the wisdom, in debate,
Of Sages, sent from every STATE,
Not all the wreathes *Napoleon* gained,
Nor all the realm o'er which he reigned
Ere *Austria* from his league withdrew,
And Fortune from his standard flew;
Not honors by *Virginia* done,
To talk with men like JEFFERSON;
Not *Carolina's* fields of rice,
Not *Florida*, that paradise,
Not half *Missouri*, at my will,
SHOULD TEMPT ME FROM MY DOMICIL.

To this the *answer* was not long,
'Twas the mere echo of a song.
Addressed to one, who, did he hear,
Would still have turned the deafened ear.—
Salem secure, not overawed,
Grimacing, only—hemmed and hawed.

To a Young Friend, With Some Maple Sugar

Fond of her country—will my Mary please
To taste her sweets produced from Maple trees:
Which Heaven profusely planted thro' the wild
Indulgent unto man—his favorite child:
Which grace the Western woods—infit for Cane,
That loves exclusively a southern plain.
Exempt from ills their heated climes produce,
In health we gain the sweet nectarean juice:
There—slaves, deprived of all that man holds dear,
Are urged to toil by whips and blows severe.
Here cheerful freemen with their infant train,
Exult in labor, sure of honest gain
Tho' dark the colour yet no stain appears,
No trace of blood, no vestiges of tears.—
For this no seaman seeks a distant land,
And meets with shipwreck on a foreign strand,
Exposed to fevers and tornado's sway,
And pirates dreadful on the wat'ry way:
But safe in waggons, with a joyful heart,
The patient Cater seeks the distant mart.
Let other nymphs their wasteful hours prolong
In midnight dances, music, and in song—
Music and song in ancient times assigned
To praise the benefactors of mankind.
Now, prostituted vile conspire their aid
In injuring the healthful blooming maid.
May'st thou be favored by the Power Divine,
And health, good humor, peace, be ever thine.

The Youth of the Mind

When FRANKLIN,[1] old and bowed with years,
   Felt every nerve unstrung,
His eyes bedimmed and deaf his ears,
A sophist made this odd remark,
   "If to his eye the world is dark,
     "If he is old
     "And blood is cold,
   "His mind is always young."

The sage remark I noted down,
   But scarcely could believe,
For men I deem'd of high renown,
Like common men descend the hill,
Subject, like them, to dotage, 'till
   In death's repose
   Their days they close
And slumber in the Grave.

When, now, he reach'd his eightieth year
   I call'd upon the sage,
Admired to see, rejoiced to hear,
That all was true the Sophist said:
I saw his frame, his sight decayed,
   But in his mind
   Did clearly find
Him thirty years of age.

And hence an argument I draw
   That *mind* can never die:
The Body yields to nature's law,
But *that*, which animates the frame,
Forever lives, and is the same,
Whether it stray through empty space,
Whether it has, or has no place,
   —'Tis young to all Eternity.

---

[1] Dr. Franklin was born in 1708 and died April, 1790.

Prologue to Kotzebue's Play

When *Shakespeare's* fires illumed a barbarous age,
Wit, judgement, genius, joined to adorn the stage;
The new formed scene admiring thousands drew
Its magic charmed them, and the charm was new.
The rugged heart to savage manners chained,
Was by the stage to gentler habits trained;
It glowed, it felt, and passion's milder sway
Calmed the rude bosom in some well wrought PLAY,
The breast, that ne'er had beat with loves refined,
Hence taught, its frozen apathy resigned;
A polished nation rose on virtue's plan,
To prove the stage might form the social man.

If such the case two centuries ago,
As Time's long annals, uncontested show,
How much indebted to those bards we stand,
Whose lamps first blazed, to civilize a land,
Taught man with man to form the social tie,
The first grand link in nature's harmony;—
Blest be their memory, who thus early rose,
And changed to friends whom madness turned to foes.

This night, ye fair ones of our favored isle,
We ask your favor as we court your smile;
This night, ye manly Patron of the Stage,
May our best efforts your applause engage,
In this fair dome, that boasts your *Hero's* NAME,
A chief immortal in the roles of fame,
Of your kind favors let us claim our share,
Forget, at reason's feast, your daily care,
To one, deserving of your aid, extend
The hand of friendship, *and be proved his friend:*
A play we give of sentiment refined,
At once that soothes and meliorates the mind.

The Thespian Muse will do her part to please,
Correct with grace, and dignified with ease,
To all who come, fine sentiment impart,
Delight the fancy, and improve the heart;
Proud, if she finds *Columbia's* sons engage
To rear, protect, and animate the stage,
Still to endure, chaste, noble, and sublime,
The shafts of envy and the blasts of time.

The Military Ground

The Hills remain!—but scarce a man remains
  Of all, who once paraded on these lands,
Yet the rough soil some vestiges retains
  Of camps, and crowds, and military bands.
I mark, I trace a spot renowned in fame,
  And something, still, may Fancy's pencil claim.

Here walked the man, to live to distant times,
  Born, to a world its freedom to restore,
While 'midst a war of rancour and of crimes,
  Fell at his feet the shafts of foreign power;
And *they,* who trod this verge of Hudson's stream,
  Won all he wished, with duty, love, esteem.

To raise such scenes, pourtray such crimes again,
  To draw the picture of a land distressed,
Another Gage should cross the *Atlantic* main,
  Another Navy float on *Hudson's* breast,
Some new *Cornwallis* to the charge return,
  Burgoyne arrive, and *Howe* for conquest burn.

Here flamed the fires that flash'd beyond the wave
  And struck with anguish, terror, and despair
The *Chiefs* who little to their monarch gave
  But sky built castles, and the brow of care:
Manhattan's island saw their rise and fall,
  To dine on wormwood, and to sup on gall.

Ambition's aims, with hateful avarice join'd
  Would worlds subdue, if worlds could yet be found,
Bend to one Yoke the myriads of mankind
  Debase their tribes, & chain them to the ground:
To *such* the muse her offerings will disdain,
  Nor shall they live in her celestial strain.

This vision, life!—how cheerly, once, was trod
　This glittering field, when all was mirth and glee,
Their views accomplished, and their fame abroad,
　And *Patriots*, still, though curs'd with *Poverty*.
Naught are they now—all decomposed to clay,
　Or wrecks of men, and hastening to decay.

The vulture screams!—approaching night I see,
　This scene of Soldiers soon will be concealed,
Where, once, perhaps, they met at yonder tree,
　Where, once, no doubt, my friend, like us they smiled
To think that *George*, the terror of mankind,
　Here, to another *George* a world resign'd.

On the Loss of the Packet Ship Albion.
Captain Williams, of New York.

As near the cliffs of old Kinsale,
The Albion plough'd her desperate way,
From Southern skies a threatning Gale
Howl'd through her shrouds, and sung dismay;
Though boisterous seas her flands assail'd
No spirit droop'd or efforts fail'd.

On weathering this too fatal shore,
The land a lee predicted ills,
Presaging she should see no more
Dear Sandy Hook, or Jersey Hills;
    No more Manhattan's isle review,
    The port from which at first she flew.

The Heavens in black their stars with-held,
A morning carpet veil'd the sky,
The hovering clouds in mists counceal'd
The reefs so near, and rocks so high.
    What, now, was skill? what skill could do,
    Was try'd, and strength and vigour too.

"Cheer up, my friends," the captain said,
"We yet may shun the dangers near,
Where morning dawn shall be displayed,
The gale may break, the heavens may clear;
    And then we soon Old England greet,
    With wind abaft and flowing sheet!"

The word was given—the yards were braced,
The bowlines haul'd, she dash'd away;
Well trim'd, the high black wave she faced
In hopes to gain St. George's sea;
    Her well known station to attain,
    And ride on Mercey's stream again.

That instant, from distracted skies,
The gallant Albion felt a blast,
That human power or force defies.
And made a wreck of every mast;
   With what a shock I grieve to tell,
   Her spars were broke, her cordage fell!

'Twas then the worthy Williams said,
"Dear comrades, I command no more!
Our doom is fixed, the swelling tide
Impels our barque to yonder shore,
   And there, as none appear to save,
   My noble ship must find a grave—
   Yes—there with all her costly freight
   My gallant Albion meets her fate.

A floating mass, a hulk she lies,
She takes her last tremendous roll,
Our Fortune every hope denies
To shun the reef or clear the shoal:
   No help, no friend, no safety nigh,
   'Tis our's to yield and ours to die!"

He spoke—she struck, with thundering sound,
Then shrieks were heard that rent the sky,
And total ruin stalk'd around;
But, soon was hush'd each fearful cry,
   When o'er them burst the last high wave
   To all, or most, a watery grave!

To a Young Farmer

To CAMBRIA's College *sent astray*,
   You leave a mass of WORK behind
Science calls, her call obey,
   She gives a polish to the mind,
For *there* is learned what *Euclid* taught,
And *Plato* dreamed, and *Newton* thought.

Seven years of youth are far too much
To study *Greek*, or study *Dutch;*
And yet, the *lust*, some people shew,
Is the most useful of the two.

None writ a better style than HE [1]
Who fought us into Liberty;
And yet, to Linguists be it known,
He knew no language but his own.

The *diamond*, from its dark abode,
   Is worth the care to polish well;
But *pebbles* on the turnpike road,
   Tho' polished, none would buy or sell:
To polish *such* would be no crime,
But surely, truly,—loss of time—
To *crust* the road is all their end,
Nor farther Nature did intend.

Released from care, from labors free,
   In College Glooms *who* turns recluse
May know what *Grecians* termed a TREE,
   And what the old Romans called a GOOSE:
With empty sounds he feeds his mind,
And not the knowledge of mankind—

[1] Washington.

Nor even THE KNOWLEDGE OF THE SOIL,
   Transcending all that man can know;
The ART that makes the kettle boil,
   The art that bids the harvests grow,
The art of arts, that never fails,
That fills the dish, and swells the sails.

By poring long on bulky *Tomes,*
   The labors of the honored dead,
The shallow brain a pride assumes
   That proves, indeed, a vacant head.
The brightest wits are glad to own
They know—how little can be known.

The slippers red, the morning gown,
   I like them not—away! away!
The soft *mattress* and *beds* of *down*
   Should be exchanged for *beds of hay,*
Where *Labor* finds a sounder nap
Than *Sloth,* indulged on pleasure's lap.

The silken gloves, the lady's hand,
   May do for students, pale and thin;
But YOU—foredoomed to till the land
   With sweat of brow, and many a grin,
Take care your paws are better stuff
And near a-kin to *Adam's* Buff.[2]

[2] Leather made of Buffaloe's hide.

To a Young Person Addicted to the Gaming Table

Nullem numen abest si sit Prudentia præsens.

To build your hopes on Fortune's wheel
    Is folly in the extreme,
Deceitful as a harlot's smile,
    Delusive as a dream:
Ah, let the cards, the dice, alone,
That wealth ensure to few or none.

Too often to your *trembling* hand
    Eudocia deals, *Eudocia* plays,
In hopes to knot the *marriage* band,
    And with you pass her *halcyon* days:
A thousand TRICKS she wears, with ease,
And yet, in every *trick*, can please.

If sense, or reason swayed her heart,
    She must despise your play;
Would rather see you drive a cart
    Than first-rate Gambler of the day:—
Esteem that from discernment springs,
And *Jack* of *Clubs*, are different things.

An ancient *Sage* at *Athens* said
    "If prudence we possess,
No other DEITY we need
    To work our happiness"—
And, for a *Stoick*, he said true,
In *Grecian* style, in Reason's view

One Goblet brings another on,
    To cheer you when you lose;
The sharper asks your *watch* in pawn
    For what he counts his dues:

Observing this, as people will,
They hold you—travelling *down the hill!*

I saw you sip your glass of *Gin,*
   I heard you fret and brawl:
But they who lose, and they who win,
   In truth, are *losers* all:—
They lose their time, they lose their fame,
And money leaves them—as it came.

Instead of asking, what's the hour?
   You sat in doleful dumps;
And ask your Partner, looking sour,
   You asked him, *What is Trumps?*—
The *clock* went on, not fast or slow,
But often said, 'Tis time to go!

The wakeful night, the drowsy day
   Is not in Nature's scheme;
Does she her solar orb display
   That man may doze and dream,
Exclude the light, for sloth disposed
On beds of *down,* with windows closed!

Their purpose thus if *some* pursue
   Take warning by their fate,
Their minds are soured, their days are few,
   And Bailiffs round them wait,
To shew the effects of wasted years,
And fill Eudocia's eyes with tears.

Philosophical Fortitude

Though Vice and Folly dread that final day
Which takes us from this dying world away,
Yet no weak fears of mingling with the dust
Alarm the Virtuous or disturb the Just;
Let systems fail, or systems be restored,
Still, active Virtue meets a due reward.—
Though Vice and Folly dread that debt to pay
Required by Nature on the funeral day,
Yet conscious goodness soars above the clod
And life, well spent, secures the path to God.

    The Wise at Nature's Laws will ne'er repine,
Nor think to scan, or mend the grand design.
Ills from ourselves, and not from Nature flow,
And true Religion never leads to woe:
What Nature gives, receive—her laws obey,
If you must die to morrow, live to day:
'Tis ours to improve this life, not ours to know
From whence this *meteor* comes, or where shall go,
This *mind*, this *spark*, that animates our frame,
Directs, impels, and still remains the same.—
As o'er some fen, when heaven is wrapt in night,
An *ignus fatuus* waves its trembling light;
Now up, now down, the mimic taper plays,
As varying winds affect the trembling blaze;
Soon the light phantom spends its magic store,
Dies into darkness, and is seen no more:
Thus flows our life! but is that life secure?—
Heaven trusts no mortal's fortune in his power,
Nor serve those prayers, importunate, we send,
To alter *fate* or *Providence* to mend;
As well in *Judgement* as in *mercy* kind,
Heaven hath, for both, the fittest state designed,

The *fools* on life, the *wise*, on death depend,
Waiting, with sweet reverse, their toils to end;
Quit the vain scene, where few have found or know
The first grand purpose—*why we live below.*

General Lefevre Denouette

Ships to conduct, or Oceans to control,
  Phenician arts, once more, to bring to view,
Requires a daring, but a patient soul
  Inured to dangers and to miseries too;
To meet the worst, with firm enduring mind,
  Calm even in death, in fates last shock resigned.

When the proud ALBION struck the fatal reef
Where pitying crowds could yield her no relief,
With *those,* to friendship, friends, and country lost,
Lefevre perished on that iron coast,
  Where cliffs, tremendous, swept by many a gale,
  Mark the rude entrance to thy port, *Kinsale.*

Fortune, to some in clouds and glooms arrayed
Paints Life's career with one unmingling shade,
No smiles, no ray of Sunshine through the gloom
Alleviates the pain, or mitigates their doom;
  Shade follows shade, to disconcert the *man,*
  And the dark circle ends as it began.

Such was thy lot, Lefevre, such thy fate,
Napoleon's favorite at no distant date;
Such was thy doom!—"inglorious some would say
"Better in dungeons to have pined away,
  "Better in arms to find an honored grave
  "Than sink, unnoticed, in the briny wave."

They speak not so who drink at wisdom's spring,
Their cool reflection says a different thing:
When the great author of our life decrees
The final hour, and seals our destinies,
  Alike to HIM—*they* equal honor claim
  Who sink in oceans or in fields of fame.

But still, we hold Lefevre's doom severe,
Almost in view of all he held most dear;
With joy returning to a wife adored,
An infant offspring, country, friends, restored,
   Just in the hour when all his hopes ran high
   Just on the verge of France—fate bade him die!

Twice had his *consort* sought *Columbia's* shore,
To meet the man she early loved, once more;
Twice ruthless tempests made the ships a wreck;
And to her native Europe forced her back;
   While he, an Exile in our western waste
   Her long lost image in his dreams embraced.

Sighed as he toil'd, and gazed from day to day,
In Fancy's visions o'er the watery way:
Her wish'd arrival every toil endeared.
For *her* he ploughed the soil, the forest cleared;
   For *her*, the solace of his six year's pain,
   Whom heaven had doomed him—not to meet again.

Oh! hadst thou stayed in *Alabama's* waste
And her dear form in Fancy's dreams embraced,
Hope still had beamed upon thy night of gloom;
Exile was better than a *watery* tomb—
   Now every hope, to cheer the mind is fled,
   For one is wretched, and the other dead!

On the Civilization of the Western Aboriginal Country

Strange to behold, unmingled with surprize,
Old hights extinguished, and new hights arise,
Nature, herself, assumes a different face,—
Yet such has been, and such will be the case.
Thus, in the concave of the heavens around,
Old stars have vanished, and new stars been found,
Some stars, worn out, have ceased to shine or burn,
And some, relumed, to their old posts return.

Two wheels has Nature constantly for play,
She turns them both, but turns a different way;
What one creates, subsists a year, an hour,
When, by destructions wheel is crushed once more.
No art, no strength this wheel of fate restrains,
While matter, deathless matter, still remains,
Again, perhaps, now modelled, to revive,
Again to perish, and again to live!

THOU, who shalt rove the trackless western wastes
Tribes to reform, or have new *breeds* embraced,
Be but sincere!—the native of the wild
If wrong, is only Nature's ruder child;
The arts you teach, perhaps not ALL amiss,
Are arts destructive of domestic bliss,
The *Indian world,* on Natures bounty cast,
Heed not the future, nor regard the past.—
They live—and at the evening hour can say,
We claim no more, for we have had one day.
The *Indian* native, taught the ploughman's art,
Still drives his oxen, with an *Indian* heart,
Stops when they stop, reclines upon the *beam,*
While briny sorrows from his eye-lids stream,

To think the ancient trees, that round him grow,
That shaded *wigwams* centuries ago
Must now descend, each venerated bough,
To blaze in fields where nature reign'd till now.

Of different mind, he sees not with your sight,
Perfect, perhaps, as viewed by Nature's light:
By Nature's dictates all his views are bent,
No more *imperfect* than his AUTHOR meant.

All moral virtue, joined in one vast frame,
In 'forms though varying, still endures the same;
Draws to one point, finds but one central end,
As bodies to one common centre tend.

Whether the impulse of the mind commands
To change a *creed,* or speculate in lands,
No matter which—with pain I see YOU go
Where wild Missouri's turbid waters flow,
There to behold, where simple Nature reign'd,
A thousand *Vices* for one *Virtue* gained;
Forests destroyed by *Helots,*[1] and by slaves,
And forests cleared, to breed a race of knaves—
The bare idea clouds the soul with gloom—
Better return, and plough the soil at home.

But, if devoid of subterfuge, or art,
You act from mere sincerety of heart,
If honor's ardor in the bosom glows
Nor *selfish* motives on *yourselves* impose,
Go, and convince the natives of the west
That *christian* morals are the first and best;
And yet *the same* that beam'd thro' every age,
Adorn the *ancient,* or the modern page;
That without which, no social compacts bind,
Nor *honor* stamps her image on mankind.

[1] All of servile conditions among the ancient Athenians were denominated *Helots.*

Go, teach what Reason dictates should be taught,
And learn from *Indians* one great Truth you ought,
That, though the world, wherever man exists,
Involved in darkness, or obscured in mists,
The *Negro*, scorching on *Angola's* coasts,
Or *Tartar*, shivering in *Siberian* frosts;
Take all, through all, through nation, tribe, or clan,
The child of Nature is the *better* man.

Lines Written at Demarest's Field

In quest of honour, wealth, promotion, fame,
　　One fatal step his prospects blasted all;
In pride of youth he met a death of shame,
　　While pitying thousands mourn'd his early fall:
War's iron laws condemned him to that doom
That most experience, who such masks assume.

A *Traitor's* avarice led him to that fate
　　Which all bemoaned, when on the cruel tree,
He saw ambition's madness, saw too late
　　One step too far, to vanquish Liberty.
Death he despised, and boldly lead the storm,
Nor feared his *exit,* but abhorred the form.

Weak was the *project* British *wisdom* laid
　　To work one ruin, and the STATES subdue:
Had *Andre's* fortune seen West Point betrayed,
　　Fort *Putnam* lost, and *Arnold* with it, too,
Our young Republics might have scorn'd it all,
Have seized their castle and reclaimed the wall.

John Andre's bones from forty years repose [1]
　　Now disinterred, repass the Atlantic deep:
Now pomp and pride a costlier tomb bestows,
　　Destined with *heroes,* and with *kings* to sleep.
Peace to them all—Tappan her charge restores
To moisten British eyes on British shores!

[1] The Body was buried near the place of execution in October, 1779.

Verses Written on Leaving a Great House Of Much Ceremony, but Little Sincerity, Or Hospitality

"This is not mine ain house,
Ken by the rigging o't,"
ALLAN RAMSAY.

CAUTION

Thou, who shalt halt at Beaurepaire,
  On business, or for pleasures sake,
Please to observe some folks are there
  Who notice every step you take,
    Survey your *hat,* inspect your *shoes,*
    But not *omission* will excuse.

You comb your hair, you brush your coat
Almost to thread-bare to the neat,
Yet, in its *knap* a single spot
Will be observed by all you meet:
    And you will be no more caress'd,
    But censured as a *clown* at best.

If hungry as a famished hawk,
You dare not fill your craving maw,
Or sure to be the country talk,
The laughing stock of high and low:
    Be on your guard at every meal,
    And starve to death to be *genteel.*

Good heaven! what a *Lord* I dreamt—!
The *Lordling* of this House, who sees,
Must see, with feelings of contempt,
An insect shivering in the breeze,
    Such creatures, in a wintry day,
    A north-west wind would blow away.

The *Angels,* who in habit *here,*
Were Angels not ten years ago:
I knew them in a humble sphere,—
But see, what *sudden wealth* can do!
  It looks at things with other eyes,
  And *new ideas* strangely rise.

I knew them ere their pride begun,
I knew them when of *manners plain;*
When *Julia* wash'd, and *Susan* spun,
And *pewter plates* were scoured by *Jane;*
  When giant *Jacob* drove the *plough*
  He would not wish to hear of—*now.*

Ah, well-a-day! how many dreams
A lofty house makes *mighty men*—
How gay these fluttering females seem
That wore a course *home-spun*—I knew when:
  But *now!*—to please both *White & Black,*
  A man must be—*a man of wax.*

Lo! *linsey woolsey* changed to *silk*—
They almost *speak,* and *look* divine;
Madeira laughs at *Butter milk,*
For *twelve* at noon at *six* they dine;
  They cheat in periods of a mile,
  And folly marks their swelling style.

A curse on such preposterous whims!
And why a moment tarry there,
Where glittering *Bucks* and madam *Prims*
Disgusted me with *Beaurepaire;*
  A mansion that may suit the vain,
  At which I shall not halt again?

Oh for the hut of Indian *Sam!*
He dwells in yonder woods, they say:
His buckwheat meal and venison ham
Once more would cheer me on my way.
    I'll seek him, be it far or near,
    To find a welcome more sincere.

Verses on an Upper Street Physician

Some choose to fly, for well they know
In silent mansions under ground,
Those last abodes to which we go,
No longer sensual joys are found:
No splendid feasts, no flowing bowls
Smile on the megre feast of souls!

In fighting fields who quits his post
Of fame or valor does not boast;
On stormy seas who skulks below
A seaman's duty does not know,
Or, if he knows, he has no heart,
No soul, to act the seaman's part.

Sangrado!—why this sudden flight?
Or, can you think *retreating* right,
When every art should be essayed,
When all your skill should be displayed
To check those fires you might restrain,
That carry death through every vein.

Three days ago *Monismia* died,
In flower of Youth, and beauty's pride;
No *Galen* near her couch she found,
No *Sydenham*, rever'd, renown'd,
No *Rush*, who once adorned our land,
Prince of the Esculapian band,
But beardless boys, raw from the schools,
And hardly versed in Buchan's [1] rules.

Had you remain'd, and faced the foe
(This *scythe of death*, this morbid glow,

[1] Author of a well-known book, or system, of medical practice, called the **Family Physician.**

76

This plague of plagues, that acts unseen,
This *giant* from the *Quarantine*)
Who knows but *she* (regretted maid!)
Had lived, to *bless you* for your aid:—
   The chance is past—she sleeps in peace,
   But *your* remorse shall never cease.

If yet your face admits a blush,
If still, with tears your eyes can gush,
Restrain them not: resume your *post,*
And strive to sooth *Monima's* ghost,
Which, now, may haunt your nightly dreams
And cast a gloom on future schemes;—
   Like her's, your days may yet be few,
   And you may fall by *doctors* too.

In years of health, when all was gay,
And plague and fevers far away,
When slight complaints attacked her frame
Almost officiously you came;
You felt her pulse, prescribed her *cure*
And drained her blood, to make it sure:
   But when this *deadly foe* advanced,
   You shunn'd her street—and off you danced!

To all who teach the *healing art,*
One serious truth we might impart;
With all their lectures, all their rules,
With all the science of their schools,
   With all the learning they pursue
   Let *Fortitude* be studied too.

Napoleon, freedom to restore,
Had fathom'd *all* the depths of war,
All *Caesar's* skill, what *Marlborough* knew,
He travelled the dark circle through:

With *all* their knowledge in his brain,
And *all* experience could attain,
Had he not been above *all* fear,
(Contempt of death, his character)
He had not gained his high renown,
Nor *all* his *tactics*—won the crown.

Lines to a Lady

A custom has come up, of late,
Of making presents to the GREAT:
They send a turkey, or a hen,
To—who might better give them TEN

For *Persia's* king, at *Ispahan* [1]
A splendid present you prepare:
But tell us, madam, where's the man
That will engage to take it *there?*—
It is a *monstrous* way to go,
And *cash* is rather scarce, you know.

The Prince that fills the Persian throne,
And reigns ten thousand miles away,
Has, surely, CARPETS of his own,
His subjects weave him every day—
Then, why employ such pains and care
In *presents*, to be sent so far?

To waste your time for NADIR SHAH,
Is but a wild, romantic scheme;
He is a prince *above the Law,*
His very nod is all supreme;
And presents that an *Envoy* brings,
He only takes from Brother Kings.

Are there not folks *beneath your nose,*
(Not Fortune's favorites, we may swear)
The children of *distress* and *woes,*
That ask your pity, claim your *care?*—

[1] The Capital City of Persia, and seat of the Royal Government, and residence.

79

For *such* exert your *generous* paw,
And think no more of NADIR SHAH.[2]

[2] It seems to augur ill to *Republicanism*, to observe so many of our citizens courting familiarity with, and rendering themselves obsequious to Royalists and crowned heads. Thus, not more than a year ago, was seen a Document signed, on the right hand, by *Alexander*, autocrat or despot of Russia, and on the left by Noah Worcester, a Massachusetts deacon. The good deacon, as a republican, which I am told he is, should have been ashamed to be seen in *such company*. Numbers of elegant presents are now preparing, it is well ascertained, to be sent to *crowned heads* in the East Indies and elsewhere. One in particular, it is said, is getting up, with all expedition, for her majesty, the queen of the Sandwich, or *O-why-hee* islands. If a holy missionary is to attend and conduct each of these munificent gifts, we shall have enough of them. How the funds of the Bible Societies will hold out, is not yet known.

The Passaick Garden

By sun or star by day or night
This Garden yields supreme delight;
It is that heaven, from ills exempt,
Of which the ancient Poets dreamt.
For here we see each flower that blows,
And here we scent each fragrant rose
That ever Nature's pencil drew,
With colours, to enchant the view.

In dewy morn, or evening's shade
When suns behind the hills are laid,
When moons a second light display
And dart the sun's reflected ray,
Who would not through this magic rove,
To enjoy the garden and the grove.

Oh what a dream might here be had
Of scenes we thought forever fled—
This must be Paradise complete,
At least, the muses favorite seat.
Could *Adam* here return with *Eve*,
And not a serpent to deceive,
She and her poor deluded swain
Might claim their native walks again.

For here we find a sweet repose,
And here a heavenly river flows:
Dame Nature here is calm and kind,
Nor has one frown that we can find:
Another system all would seem,
And so we think, or so we dream.

And here amidst the groves we see
An angel of the first degree,

With such a sweetness in her look—
And in her hand she held a book
So full of love and full of wit,
In verse and prose, that she had writ!—
She read aloud, with accent clear,
But few, or none were *there* to hear,
Her words so gracefully advanced,
So lightly through her Poems danced,
Had but one man of taste been there
To attend the readings of the Fair,
He would have shunn'd the Tavern throng,
And three times kissed her for her song.

If once a torrent here prevail'd,
And shallops through this garden sailed,
The *Rainbows* at *Passaick* falls
(Where Jersey maids sing madrigals,
Or *others* from that rocky steep
Too lately took the Lover's Leap)
Are tokens, *surely*, *clear* and *plain*,
That River will not flood again.

Had I the right to tarry here
To pass an age or spend a year,
Not all the wreathes *Napoleon* gained,
Nor all the realm o'er which he reign'd
Ere Austria from the league withdrew
And Fortune from his standard flew;
Not all the fame of *Washington*
For empires from *Old England* won,
Not all *Columbia*, every state
Should tempt me from this garden gate.
But, dear deception, cheat me not!
What demons cloud this charming spot!
What means that hoarse, discordant roar
Of stragglers, near Passiack's shore?

Here runs at large a yelping cur,
And there the Jockey—whip and spur—
To much I fear my bliss supreme
Was merely fancy's idle dream—
And now I see a Tavern nigh
That noisy beings occupy.
I see them drunk, I hear them swear,
And now for boxing they prepare,
And now they make their courage known,
And now they grunt and now they groan;
Their tongues are loud, the men are bold,
And mastiffs growl and women scold,
And drunkards reel, and children squall;
So that to take it all in all,
These and some other *little* harms,
Have robbed my *Eden* of its charms;—
If *this* be Paradise complete,
Or even the muses favorite seat,
I sieze my staff, and pray for grace
To find it in—some other place.

Bonaparte

"The latter end of the Republic forgot the beginning of it."—
TEMPEST.

Advanced to wear the Gallic Crown,
   The *Bourbon* monarch prostrate low,
The powers supreme that put him down
   May disregard *Napoleon* too:
Though guarded by a chosen band
Of chieftains, trained to his command,
   Will they prove true, will they prove true?

Yes! Fortune may be false at last,
And to the ground *Napoleon* cast:
   To speak my mind,
   She has designed
Some sudden turn in *Europe's wheel*,
   And she may turn it soon!—
Though on a throne, a height so grand,
Upon that height I would not stand
   For all below the moon.

For round him *dogs* unnumbered growl,
And distant *wolves*, still lowder, howl,
And *vultures* scream, and *tigers* roar;
And nations are disgusted more
   With *regal rank* that he assumes;
More rancour boils within the breast,
And more this sudden change detest
   Than human wisdom overcomes!

The *lost Republic* greets him not!
Her memory is a fatal blot
   On his renown, on his renown!—

He swore to keep a nation free
That had relapsed to anarchy,
He swore to guard democracy,
　　Not hurl it down, not hurl it down!

Oh, grand mistake! what can atone
For mischiefs, then so rashly done!
　　Now Europe hugs her chains:
Had France remained *republican*,
And sanctioned *there*, the RIGHTS OF MAN,
All would have been secure, and free
From tyrants and from tyranny,
　　That soon may rise again.

A Midnight Storm in the Gulph Stream

Now what avails it to be brave?—
On liquid precipices hung,
Around us fierce tornadoes rave,
Beneath us yawn'd a sea-deep grave,
And silenced every tongue.

What ruling force, what active power
That bids the winds and waves obey.
Will now appear to sooth the roar
Of nature, in her agony?

Does lightning's flash announce our doom!—
Do thunders, rattling through the sky?—
Strange fires the watery wave illume,
That inlet to eternity!

The creaking yards, the laboring masts
Proclaimed *distress,* not distant far:
No sail endures these rugged blasts,
Engaged in elemental roar.

Ah me! what waves assail the ship,
What bursting seas, what floods of spray!
Scarce nimble *Jack* retains his grip
When up the shrouds he gropes his way.

What yet avails, what yet remains
But anxious hearts, and toil severe—
The clanking pumps—incessant rain
Descend, another deluge here!

How feeble are the strongest hands,
How weak all human efforts prove!—
He who obeys, and who commands
Must await a mandate from above.

'Tis done!—we view in western skies
    The clouds dispersed, and stars appear;
Before the blast the vapour flies;
    The waves subside their awful swell,
        The *starboard* watch hails, All is well!
        And from the land again we steer.

To a Lady Remarkably Fond of Sleep

Let others dread autumnal gales
When Libra holds the balanced scales;
But you no fears, no danger know,
Why should I be concern'd for you?—

Who would slumber on the deep
That on shore might sounder sleep?—
Take your choice of sea or land,
Both are *yet* at your command;

Both have evils, plagues and care,
And, on land, *you have your share:*
Be the choice as you incline,
Terra Firma shall be mine.

Seas and skies are scenes that tire
When nothing more is to admire;
Soon we wish the land again,
Nature's variegated scene.

Let me ask you, have you *mind*
To be in every case resign'd;
Are you truly well prepared,
Never subject to be scared,

Wipe your eye, lament and squall
When danger there is none at all:
Are you proof against the shocks
Of *Greenland ice and Irish rocks?*

Dearest Jenny think of *this*,
Take my council not amiss.—
On the vast Atlantic main
Dangers lurk—a ghastly train.

There are *Pirates,* bent on plunder,
Sons of rapine, sons of thunder;
There (the *Yankees* all agree)
Swims the *Serpent of the sea.*

There the *Shark* and there the *whale*
Who might thresh you with his tail
'Till your gay, embroidered dress
Shewed its signal of distress.

There are pretty *mermaids* too
Maids, I hope as good as you,
Virgin beauties, always watch'd
Rarely seen and rarely catch'd.

On the pillow of your bed
Morpheus shall his opiates shed
Till the *seventy sixth degree*
Ends a thousand leagues of sea.

On the ocean while you ride
May your dreams be satisfied;
Be it clear or be it dreary,
May you sleep till you are weary.

On those waters while she strays
Please good *Neptune* smooth the seas;
Gentle *zephyrs,* with your pinions
Waft her o'er his rude dominions.

Never think of what I said,
Dangers seen or dangers hid;
Be we stationed where we will,
Dangers must surround us still.

Objects there are many more,
Dangers less, or dangers more,

More than Neptune's sons of art
Yet have placed on any *chart*.

To avoid them all you can
Go upon a prudent plan:
To the winds resign your cares,
With you take the churche's prayers,
Then, if dangers should dismay,
Sleep the danger all away.

The Arrival at Indian Sam's
(Or, Wee-Quali's) Wigwam

The traveller, after leaving the gaieties and
splendor of Beaurepaire, proceeds, one afternoon
in quest of Indian Sams residence in the woods.
—His reception and Conversation makes the
substance and subject of the fol-
lowing lines.

Through ups and downs, a rugged road
I steered my course for Sam's abode,
But found it not—at last the Sun
Descended to the horizon:
The people said at Beaurepaire
It lay exactly *South* from there,
Nor so remote from that abode
(Though far from any public road)
That, if I kept an Indian track,
That Indians used for ages back
I would be sure, on that blind way,
To reach him ere the close of day.

The Indian path was blind indeed,
O'er run with shrubs and hemlock weed,
My stockings torn, and scratched my face
I soon was in a shocking case;
But thanked my stars, as matters were,
I was not bound for *Beaurepaire.*

So when the shades of night came on,
And every glimpse of day was gone,
I looked above and saw the stars,
And glanced at *Jupiter* and *Mars.*
My best respects to these I paid,
Thank'd them, but wanted not their aid.

At last, I saw that gleaming star
Which sailors, most of all, revere;
The sacred star, which marks the pole,
Round which the neighbouring lanthorns roll;
Which always keeps its wonted steep
Nor hides her glory in the deep:
He shone serene, benign, and clear,
Fix'd in the tail of the little Bear,
Though some have thought, profane and blind,
A nobler place might be assigned.

On him I turn'd my back, and then,
Like thousands of ungrateful men,
Enjoy'd his help—and taught my horse
To crawl, exact, *a southward course.*

At last, amidst the mists of night,
I saw, far off, a gleam of light,
A *will a-wisp,* upon the wing,
I fear'd—a some such develish thing:
But, passing through a tuft of trees
Soft murmuring to the midnight breeze,
Conviction strong and stronger grew
That what I sought was now in view.

Approaching to the savage door
I look'd behind, and look'd before,
I looked to *east* and look'd to *west,*
And *north* and *south*—and look'd my best,
In hopes to spy some friendly hand
To black my boots and smooth my band,
To brush my hat, and darn my hose,
And lend some other help—God knows—
But recollected, in a trice,
I need not, *now* be over nice
While wandering in a forest drear,
A dozen miles from *Beaurepaire.*

An Indian dog began to bark
As if to say—"Stand off . . . 'tis dark!
None I admit to yonder yard
Till *Sam* is roused, and on his guard."

And soon a whoop assailed my ear
In words of thunder, *who comes there?*

"I am a stranger in the wilds,
And come a wondering, leagues and miles;
I come from sops, I come from fools,
I come from folks who *eat by rules.*—
From those who rise from *hopping clods*
To be advanced to demi-gods;
I come from *ladies,* newly made,
From ditchers born that shun a spade,
I come, my friend, from I know where—
I come half-starved, from *Beaurepaire!*"

"And what's your business in this wood?—
Come you for evil or for good—
You come, you say from *Beaurepaire!*—
Good man, what devil took you there?—
I sell them *game,* and let me tell you
They never pay me half the value.
They are a lofty minded sett,
Of high designs—but deep in debt—
Come in, come in!—admit him Brave [1]
The man shall eat the best I have,
And that is *squirrels* killed this day,
And *venison* roasted my own way.
I am a chief of little fame
We-quallis is my Indian name,
By *that* I am by most address'd
But *Sam's* intended for a Jest.

[1] The Indian dogs name in the Oneida language, winni-pong, or Big Captain.

To none alive I make my court,
And *otter hunting* is my sport,
That means *my name*, of long descent,
Ere white men found this continent.—
Your horses belly shall be stored
With such as Indians can afford;
I am not arm'd with tigers claws,
No scythes are planted in my haws,
And yet your books, your spies, your priests
Report us worse than savage beasts."

My horse was to a hovel led,
Dry leaves were strewed to make his bed,
And planty, straight, before him placed;
Wild oats were suited to his taste,
Or hunger made him relish well
What Indians neither buy nor sell;
He had been doom'd at *Beaurepaire*
Camelion-like to feed on air,
And, like his master, lean enough
No doubt, was pleased to scamper off.

That service done he led me in
A wigwam, free from noise and din;
On rushes slept the madam *Squaw*
Her pillow shew'd a mat of straw
And three *poppooses* [2] near her lay
All painted in the Indian way.—
The *furniture* of this abode
Would hardly make a shoulder load,
But yet enough for such as these
Whom very little serves to please;
It was not rich, and something rare,
But quite unfit for *Beaurepaire*.

Three days I pass'd with honest *Sam*,
Regaling on his venison ham,

[2] Indian children, under four years of age.

His buckwheat cakes and squirrel broth
On tables void of table cloth:
He seem'd a warrior and a sage,
And *there* I could have pass'd an age,
For all was calm, serene and free
The picture of simplicity.

And, when inclining to depart
And almost with a heavy heart;
Preparing to resume my way,
He said, "There's nothing, friend, to pay!
I shew you to the Turnpike road
Too near, alas! to this abode:
And; when returning from the town
Manhattan of such high renown,
Be it your first and greatest care
To keep aloof from *Beaurepaire;*
My heart is good—my face is plain,
You are welcome, friend, to—call again."

Circumnavigation

The Franklin, with her sails unfurled,
Wafts the *first* Lady round the world,
That, from *Columbus* to this day,
Was ever known so far to stray.

In *such a view*, who can mistake?—
She is a modern *Francis Drake;*
Who, with the patience of a Job,
First put a girdle round the Globe.[1]
Good luck!—when first she went on board,
I marked the belt of *Irion's sword:*
It shone benign—and *Noah's Dove*[2]
Not augured ill, but boded love.

But, from the vast Pacific main,
Ere *Iphigenia* comes again,
Will not her fine complexion change,
And half imbibe the olive tinge?—

Stop, *Anson,* and your journal shew—[3]
I think she sails as far as you:
Both *Tropics* have the *Franklin* seen,
And both have welcomed *Iphigene.*

To be companion to the sun,
Is not the chance of every one;—
To travel round our earthly sphere,
Would madness to that dame appear,

[1] *i.e.* The first Englishman, in the reign of Elizabeth.
[2] A Southern constellation of the stars.
[3] Lord Anson's voyage round the world, 1740-44.

Who, idly bred to walk the streets,
And smile, perhaps, on half she meets,
On *Hudson,* mostly, takes the air,
And ends her navigation *there:*

She, rather than survey new shores,
Would teaze the clerks in merchants' stores,
When to the shelves she bids them fly,
For goods, she never meant to buy:

She more regards her parlour fire,
And more it suits her *home* desire.
Than all the ardent climates known,
Or lamps that warm the torrid zone.

What female, in our cities born,
But dreads the mention of Cape Horne,
The Polar ice, barbarian states,
Magellan's clouds, *Magellan's* streights?

Not so the female we pourtray,
Who, now, upon the watery way,
Views distant isles, and shores, that we
Immured at home, can never see.

Fair lady, may you safely sail,
And may your *Chaplain's* prayers prevail,
When he, good creature, at his ease
Demands fair weather and smooth seas.

Like *Venus,* late our evening guest,
If *now* we lose you in the west,
The day may come, when from afar,
You will return, a morning star.

You will return!—and, on your way,
Some sighs of recollection pay—
You will return, and view that Isle,[4]

[4] St. Helena, Napoleon's Grave.

Where lost *Napoleon* grieved awhile,
And rests, repultured in that spot,
Where *Parma's Dutchess* heeds him not.

You will return with *Indian Teas,*
And *porcelain* from the famed *Chinese,*
And rarest products ever known,
And MONKIES, purchased at *Ceylon,*[5]
That will in every street appear,
And rival half our *Dandies* here.

[5] A large East India Island abounding with those animals.

Ode on a Remote Perspective View
of Princeton College

The expanse above no cloud deforms,
  No mists obscure the day;
So, mounting to this hill of storms,
  We take our social way.
Amanda shall partake the Glass
To observe the seniors as they pass,
Who toiling for the first degree
The time is come that sets them free,
  Dispersive of the class.

Where *Millstone's* stream, in swampy Groves
  Collects its limpid rills,
And where the infant current roves
  Amidst its parent hills,
The *Hill of pines* exalts its head,
And towering near the River's bed,
Gives many a distant sky-topt view
In coloured heights of misty blue
  In wild disorder spread.

Among the rest, but far remote,
  We *Princeton's* summit scan,
And verdent plains which there denote
  The energies of man:
By aid of art's *Perspective Glass*
O'er many a woody vale we pass;
The *glass* attracts, and brings more near
What first, to naked vision here,
  Seem'd a chaotic mass.

And there we trace, from far displayed,
  The muses favorite seat,
And groves, within whose bowery shade
  The Sons of science meet.

99

Devotion to her altars calls
In plainly decorated halls—
Those walls engage the *Athenian* muse
Where Science, still, her course pursues—
    Those venerated walls!

In *Galen's* art, who took the lead,
    That Pile was seen to rear,
And some who *preach* and some who *plead,*
    First courted *Science* there—
To meliorate the human soul,
The fiercest passions to control,
Is the great purpose *there* designed,
Where *Merit* never failed to find
    The *diplomatic Roll.*

Departed days shall we recall
    Or cancel half an age
When governed, once, at Nassau Hall
    The *Caledonian* Sage
His words still vibrate on my ear
His precepts, solemn and severe,
Alarmed the vicious, and the base,
To virtue gave the loveliest face
    That human-kind can wear.

From distant soils, and towns remote,
    Attracted by his name,
And some by land, and some afloat,
    The eager Students came.
Each swarming *hive* was on the wing
To taste his deep *Pierian* spring,
And round the LAMP, that near it hung,
While sense and reason yet were young
    They strove to merit fame.

What years on years have stole away
    Since, mirthful, there were seen

The Students of a former day
   Diverting on the Green!—
Before *Columbia* struck the blow
That humbled *Britain's* legions low;
When *Washington* was scarcely named,
Nor *Independence*, yet, proclaimed
   To mark her for a foe.

When *Christmas* came, and floods congeal
   And keen northwesters blew,
Adown the ice on springs of steel
   The sprightly Juniors flew:
They left the page of Grecian lore,
Ceased Nature's wonders to explore,
And gliding on the glassy plain,
At *Morven's* grove they paused—again
   Lost vigour to restore.

Ah, years elapsed, and seasons gone;
   And days forever fled,
When hymns were sung at early dawn,
   And sacred Lectures read!
Still Fancy hears the midnight prayer,
Monitions mild—when, free from care,
When smit with awe, the attentive train
Renounced the world, or owned it vain
   With penitential tear.

With pensive step, amidst those hills
   Who, now, are seen to stray,
Where *Stony Brook* or *Scudder's Mills*
   Engaged some vacant day?
What favourite *Laura* trips the lawn,
Enamoured of the classic gown,
Now claims acquaintance with the Muse,
And half avoids, or half pursues
   Some *Petrarch* from the town?

Farewell ye shades, farewell ye streams
   That will for ages flow,
Where *other minds* plan *other schemes*
   For *consequence* below!
This *tube* displays where, with the rest,
On *Euclid's* page not over blest,
We closed our Books, forgot our cares,
To stray where *Rocky Mountain* rears
   His weather-beaten crest.

Rude Cliff's adieu! that *craggy height*
   Too long our view confines;
We tread with more serene delight
   This pleasant *Hill of Pines,*
Where *they,* who, near its shaded base,
For years have had their dwelling place,
   Contented to retire,
Yet rarely climb its lofty brow
Or leave the axe, or quit the plough
   To adore the sacred Spire!

A Transient View of Monticello

Which most deserve, or most receive reward
The Sage's counsels, or the warrior's sword?

This building, ancient and decayed
Too plainly wants the artist's aid,
To make it as of old it stood
A hermitage within a wood
But graced with all that might display
The architecture of that day.

A thousand might the pile renew
To make it last an age or two;
The columns, now, by time defaced
By able hands might be replaced,
But who by friendship, skill, or care
The time worn owner can repair?

In years, advanced to eighty-four,
'Tis time, almost to shut the door,
To bid a troop of mourners come
To attend the body to the tomb
In earth's cold bosom to inter
The patriot, sage, philosopher,
To witness rites devoutly paid
To him whose memory cannot fade.

Oh no!—may ages intervene
Before they drop the closing scene!
(Would heaven admit so bold a prayer
What numbers would not send it *there?*)
Long be unheard the funeral bell
The last address, the long farewell,
For, when he dies, he merits all
The fame, that men immortal call,

The public grief, a nation's tears—
To him no monument it rears,
Or *that* alone which suits him best,
That generous feeling in the breast,
Familiar, to each worthy mind,
Mis acting well the part assigned.

But now behold!—the mountain shrouds
His summit in a veil of clouds!
Ah while I gaze, the honoured hill
In mists of night grows darker still;
Does this announce approaching fate?—
Prolong, ye powers, his vital date
'Till to the grave he late descends
Where every human prospect ends,
But Reason, Truth, Reflection brings
A new and nobler scene of things.

On Observing a Large Red-streak Apple

In spite of ice, in spite of snow,
In spite of all the winds that blow,
In spite of hail and biting frost,
Suspended here I see you toss'd;
You still retain your wonted hold
Though days are short and nights are cold.

Amidst this system of decay
How could you have one wish to stay?
If fate or fancy kept you there
They meant you for a *Solitaire.*
Were it not better to descend,
Or in the cider mill to end
Than thus to shiver in the storm
And not a leaf to keep you warm—
A moment, then, had buried all,
Nor you have doomed so late a fall.

But should the stem to which you cling
Uphold you to another spring,
Another race would round you rise
And view the *stranger* with surprize,
And, peeping from the blossoms say
Away, old dotard, get away!

Alas! small pleasure can there be
To dwell, a hermit, on the tree—
Your old companions, all, are gone,
Have dropt, and perished, every one;
You only stay to face the blast,
A sad memento of the past.

Would fate or nature hear my prayer,
I would your bloom of youth repair
I would the wrongs of time restrain
And bring your blossom state again:

But fate and nature both say no;
And you, though late must perish too.

What can we say, what can we hope?
Ere from the branch I see you drop,
All I can do, all in my power
Will be to watch your parting hour:
When from the branch I see you fall,
A grave we dig a-south the wall.
There you shall sleep 'till from your core,
Of youngsters rises three or four;
These shall salute the coming spring
And Red streaks to perfection bring
When years have brought them to their prime
And they shall have their summers time:
This, this is all you can attain,
And thus, I bid you, live again!

A Fragment of Bion

My verses please—I thank you, friend,
That such as you my lines commend:
But is that all?—Mere empty fame
Is but an echo of a name.
To write, was my sad destiny,
The worst of trades, we all agree.
Why should I toil upon a page
That soon must vanish from the stage,
Lest in oblivion's dreary gloom,
The immensity of things to come!—
In that *abyss* I claim no part,
Is mine, indeed!—this beating heart
Must with the mass of atoms rest,
My fancy dead, my fires repress'd.

If God, or fate to man would give
In two succeeding states to live,
The first, in pain and sorrow pass'd,
In ease, content, and bliss, the last,
I then would rack my anxious brain
With study how that state to gain;
Each day, my toiling mind employ,
In hopes to share the promised joy.

But, since to all, impartial heaven
One fleeting life has only given,
'Twere madness, sure, that time to waste
In search of joys I ne'er can taste;
My little is enough for me,
Content with mediocrity:
It never sinks into the heart
How soon from hence we all must part.
What hope can bloom on life's last stage,
When every sense declines with age,

The eye be-dimm'd, the fancy dead,
The frost of *sixty* on my head,
What hope remains?—*onc debt* I pay,
Then mingle with my native clay . . .

Answer to a Letter of Despondency

When fortune quits us, or our strength decays,
Pain is our lot, and Patience is our praise.

Few words are best—the wind blows cold,
   Christmas, they say, will soon be here:
This truth the *Almanacs* foretold;
   Whose sage predictions last—a year.

What need I say—can I forget
   Your doleful letter came by post,
By which I learn, with much regret,
   You are the next thing to a ghost.

No longer bound to distant lands,
   Pursuing wealth, to lose repose,
To the bleak winds, from barren sands
   I give the story of your woes.

The aching heart and trembling hand
   To plainly mark your gloomy page,
That gives your friend to understand
   Your time grows short upon our stage.

If gouts attack, or frosts prevail,
   Still flows for you the mineral spring,
That may in time, though doctors fail,
   A renovated system bring.

The northern *geese* have winged their way
   To feast a while at Pontchartrain,[1]
Each lengthening night, and shortening day
   To some give pleasure, others pain.

[1] A large lake in West Florida, much frequented by geese, and other wild fowl, in the winter season.

On tortured nerves, your withered frame,
  Have palsies made such rude attacks?
So thin you grow, I almost dream
  Wild geese might bring you on their backs.

Throughout this interval of time
  While torpid nature takes her rest,
Each claims the right—without a crime—
  To act the part that suits him best.

To storm upon the mountain's brow
  To some affords supreme delight;
Others contrive, they best know how,
  To spend the day, or cheat the night.

If in this whirligig of things,
  When *states* decline, or *empires* fail,
You ask, while chained to *Balls-town* springs,
  What news from Europe by the mail?

All I can tell you may have read
  Five hundred times in public print;
State news—how Britain's queen is dead,
  Divorced from hearts as hard as flint.

How George the fourth has Ireland seen,
  And drank his glass with honest *Teague,*
Has dined, perhaps, at *Aberdeen,*
  And with Scotch lassies held intrigue.

In wedlock some have joined their hands,
  Another race appears of course;
While some regret its tiresome bands
  And teaze our statesmen for divorce.

That some are hang'd I scarce need say,
  And much, no doubt, against their will;
Others are in a likely way,
  Next year, to turn the Treading Mill.

The world of news, shall I detail,
  I must transmit a long Gazette;
Your patience and your eyes would fail
  To read it half—and half forget.

Your blood yet flows in youthful veins;
  Forsake the springs while yet you can,
Trod mountain roads, and rough domains,
  And be, once more, the active man.

The *spleen* is half your sad complaint:
  Be off—reject the nauseous draft,
Which many a sinner, many a saint
  Have quaff'd, and cursed it while they quaff'd.

What can be done—what yet remains?—
  Rouse up your spirits—and if here
You choose to meet in *Shrewsbury* plains
  Your friend—stand cyder—and small beer.

Vast seas in sight; great news shall tell;
  Who can their utmost depths explore?
Who views their foam, and does not feel
  Constrained their author to adore!

Advance—a welcome frank and kind
  The *Friends* will give—nor much the worse
If, with what else you bring, they find
  A generous heart—and weighty Purse.

To a New-England Poet

Though skilled in latin and in greek,
And earning fifty cents a week,
Such knowledge, and the income, too,
Should teach you better what to do:
    The meanest drudges, kept in pay,
    Can pocket fifty cents a day.

Why stay in such a *tasteless land,*
Where ALL must on a *level* stand,
(Excepting people, *at their ease,*
Who choose the *level* where they please:)
    See IRVING gone to Britain's court
    To people of *another sort,*
    He will return, with wealth and fame,
    While *Yankees* hardly know *your* name.

Lo! he has kissed a Monarch's—hand!
Before a PRINCE I see him stand,
And with the glittering nobles mix,
Forgetting *times* of seventy-six,
While *you* with terror meet the frown
Of *Bank Directors* of the town,
    The home-made *nobles* of our times,
    Who hate the bard, and spurn his rhymes.

Why pause?—like IRVING, haste away,
To England your addresses pay;
And England will reward you well,
When you some pompous story tell
    Of British feats, and British arms,
    The *maids* of honor, and their *charms.*

Dear Bard, I pray you, take the hint,
In England what you write and print,

Republished here in shop, or stall,
Will perfectly enchant us all:
 It will assume a different face,
 And post your name at every place,
 From splendid domes of first degree
 Where *ladies* meet, to sip their tea;
 From marble halls, where lawyers plead,
 Or Congress-men talk loud, indeed,
 To huts, where evening clubs appear,
 And 'squires resort—to guzzle Beer.

On a Widow Lady
(Very Rich and Very Penurious.)

Et genus et virtus nisi cum re
Vilior alga est.

If you have not money, your ancestry and personal virtues are
not worth a straw.

Wine, women, and the *strength of kings,*
Of old, were thought most potent things;
But times are changed, we must allow,
For MONEY is most powerful NOW.

'Tis *this* that makes the *Lawyer* plead,
'Tis this that makes the *Lecturer* read,
'Tis this that makes the *Parson* preach,
'Tis this that makes the *Tutor* teach,
'Tis this that bids *Physicians* study
The anatomy of the human body,
And all their skill exert to cure
The pains and plagues that men endure.

'Tis *this* that makes the maiden spin,
'Tis this that makes the gamester grin,
'Tis this that bids *Clodhopper* toil
And *marl* his fields, to improve the soil;
'Tis this that makes the Steam Boat sail
And gives her freightage—many a bale—
'Tis this that bids the cannon roar,
And vomit death from shore to shore,
Gives vigor to the wasting fire
When armies sink and crowds expire—
'Tis this that makes the wheel go round
(Whatever wheel, wherever found)

114

'Tis this that sends the ships to sea;
For this we fell the forest tree,
For this the weaver plies his loom,
For this we scribblers drive the *plume*.
It gives more *brilliancy* to fools
Than all the learning of the schools.—
In short, from *this*, and *this* alone,
The business of the world goes on—
Without a *motive* such as *this*,
The world would be a stagnant mass,
A putrid Lake, whose exhalations
Would poison and extirpate nations.

    What has been said, no doubt, is true,
Yet money cannot *all things* do—
It cannot make the globe turn round,
It cannot make false doctrine sound,
It cannot make a fool a wit,
It cannot make a clown polite:—
Dame nature's debt it cannot pay,
Nor cold *December* change to *May;*
It cannot make a miser rich,
It cannot give a monkey speech:
What can it yet not farther do?
IT CANNOT MAKE ME FOND OF YOU.

On the Death of Robert Fulton

Rest, FULTON, *here* where *Hudson's* passing wave
Rolls near your silent vault, too early grave!
Here, if some artist roves, I see him tread
Respectful near the ashes of the dead:
Here, will he say, beneath this arch, this sod,
Chills the warm heart, changed to the valley's clod,
Here, mouldering into dust, the inventive brain
No more inventive, shall with dust remain;
Here, will he say, while grief his heart devours
Here lies the man who searched through nature's powers
Proved to mankind what *active thought* can do,
And taught a system useful, great, and NEW.

None could, like him, resist bold Hudson's stream:
By powerful impetus of imprisoned steam;
By this the FULTON stems the opposing brine,
Majestic fabric, as of grand design;
By this we see the PARAGON advance,
And NEPTUNE's CAR flies o'er the long expanse;
The watery world before her prow divides,
She dares all tempests, and subdues all tides.
The RICHMOND [1] left the river and the bay,
And through fierce tempests forced her rapid way;
No canvas aids her on the billowy waste,
No gales detain her, and no tides arrest.

Who knows—can tell, where art and genius cease?—
Time from the unyielding yard may *sails* release;
When a *new race* another century hails,
Who knows but Fulton's steam o'er seas prevails!
Who knows but art such proud improvement brings;
Navies may fly without the aid of wings.
In days to come, (perhaps *our* age, may know,)
Round the vast globe, impelled by steam, they go,

[1] On her voyage to Virginia.

Bear wars loud thunder o'er the Atlantic foam,
And waft all commerce in the years to come.

Far to the western wilds this power extends;
To steams vast force old *Mississippi* bends;
A thousand leagues against his giant force
Vapour propels *flotillas* on their course;
Through many a grove, by many a savage isle
The incessant wheel drives on the unwieldy pile.
Then, Fulton, rest! thy memory shall survive
While man is grateful, or his offspring live.
And they, who on our Hudson's waters sail,
And dread no mischief from the impending gale,
These, these will say, when passing near your tomb,
The world's great Artist sleeps in yonder gloom!—

And thousands, still, shall hold his memory dear,
The *man of thoughts,* who sleeps all honored here,
Whose bold designs, on every mind impressed,
An *Archimedes* is by all confessed.
Perhaps his equal will not soon be seen,
An age at least, nay more, may intervene
Ere one, like *Fulton,* rises to our view,
And gives at once the USEFUL, GREAT, and NEW.

General De la Fayette
On His Expected Visit to America

To you, Fayette, in fair *Auvergne,*
    The muses would their homage pay;
Where yet, with deep regret, they learn,
    You pass life's closing day:
Of the great actors on our stage,
Of warrior, patriot, statesman, sage,
How few remain, how few remain!
Among the first, you claim esteem,
The historian's and the poet's theme.

May these bold waves that lash the shore,
    Succeeded by ten thousand more,
Bring on their surge that man from France,
    Who, like some hero in romance,
        Came *here,* our early wars to aid,
        And *here* unsheath'd the martial blade.

In such a task might gods engage—
    Then, all was doubtful, all was rage,
And civil discord, at its height,
    Lent wings, to speed the fiends of night:
        Then was the time to work *their* shame,
        Whom none but *Washington* could tame.

With far-famed chiefs and high bred lords,
In prime of youth you measured swords:
At those, who aw'd a trembling world,
Your dart was aim'd, your spear was hurl'd,
    Nor ceas'd your ardor, when from high,
    The tempest of the times went by:

Your efforts, added to our own,
And greatest, still, when most alone,

Gave spirit to our brilliant cause,
Saved thousands from the Lion's jaws,
   And lent us when *Cornwallis* fell,
   Assurance firm, that ALL WAS WELL.

Your conflicts with a foreign band,
Who scour'd the seas and scourg'd the land,
At this late hour, we may renew,
And own with pride, and wonder too,
   That *such a man,* in such dark days,
   Soar'd far above all human praise.

I see him with an eagle's speed,
Fly, to be where the bravest bleed,
I see him through Virginia chase
The legions of a hostile race,
   Who, proudly bent on vast designs,
   Sent navys here—to guard their lines!

Where'er they march'd, where'er they met,
They found it death to face Fayette;
Where'er they fought, where'er they flew,
Their prowess fail'd, their danger grew:—
   A traitor's [1] aid they poorly priz'd,
   Abhorr'd, detested, and despis'd.

Approach! appear that welcome day,
That sees the *Marquis* on his way;
Some ship, with ev'ry sail unfurl'd,
Parading o'er the watery world;
While lesser barques, in fleets, advance,
To hail her from her briny dance;
When from these shores we shall descry
Columbia's banner, streaming high,
And *there* in golden letters placed
A NAME, by ages undefaced;—

[1] Arnold.

And *here* be fixed his *last retreat,*
And *here* be all his hopes complete:—
May he his native *France* forget
FOR THE ADOPTED COUNTRY OF FAYETTE.

Stanzas Made at the Interment of a Sailor

Beneath this tree, below these stones
   We bury one who died at sea:
For fear the Sharks would gnaw his bones,
   Our captain lashed the helm a-lee,
     And luffing up, Tortuga near,
     He thought it right to anchor here.

In early youth, this seaman bold,
   With Captain *Cooke,* faced many a gale:
On frozen seas endured all cold,
   Where *Boreas* rends the stiffening sail;
     Then ranging, south, a smoother sea,
     Why did they name it *O-why-hee!* [1]

Thou, stranger, who shalt pass this way,
   Respect these stones that mark this grave:
Some tribute to *his* memory pay
   Who, now, no longer stems the wave,
     But sleeps, where dreams recall no more
     His absent friends, or native shore.

To traverse our terraqueous globe,
   Was the first effort of his mind;
In weather foul, in weather fair,
   He stood to every chance resigned:—
     A sea philosopher they say,
     He never cursed one stormy day.

Like Grecians old, in Homer's days,
   Above his grave we plant an *oar,*
Whose painted blade from high displays,
   This sailor's name—JAMES BARRYMORE,

[1] O-why-hee—An island in the North Pacific, or great Western Ocean, where the celebrated circumnavigator, Cooke, was slain by the savages in 1779.

121

A sailor, to old Neptune dear,
Complete in all—hand, reef, and steer.

And if these simple lines can live,
As some have lived that live no more,
They may the serious tidings give,
That on this distant sun burnt shore,
Rests one, who, manly, brave and free,
Finds home beneath a Tamarind tree.

Such honor is to James assign'd—
This humble grave let all revere,
Such as *some Commodores* may find
When time has ended their career.

Winter

The Sun hangs low!—So much the worse, we say,
For *those* whose pleasure is a Summer's day;
Few are the joys which stormy Nature yields
From blasting winds and desolated fields;
Their only pleasure in that season found
When orchards bloom and flowers bedeck the ground.

But, are no Joys to these cold months assign'd?
Has winter nothing to delight the Mind?
No friendly Sun that beams a distant ray,
No Social Moons that light us on our way?—
Yes, there are Joys that may all storms defy,
The chill of Nature, and a frozen Sky.

Happy with wine we may indulge an hour;
The noblest beverage of the mildest power.
Happy, with Love, to solace every care,
Happy with sense and wit an hour to share;
These to the mind a thousand pleasures bring
And give to winter's frosts the smiles of spring,
Above all praise pre-eminence they claim
Nor leave a sting behind—remorse and shame.

Appendix

The following poems, which appeared unsigned between 1821 and 1824, seem to me so distinctively in Freneau's manner that I, personally, do not hesitate to attribute them to him. Lacking demonstrable proof of his authorship, however, I hesitate to make strong claims for their authenticity. Perhaps a detailed investigation of rhetorical structure, rime words, and repeated phrases might render a tentative attribution more sound. But I may be forgiven, I hope, for wondering if the results of such a study would either be worth the pains or really intelligible to anyone but the investigator. Unless otherwise indicated, the following poems appeared in the *True American*.

"On the Cession of East and West Florida, from Spain to the United States," July 21, 1821 (See Lewis Leary, "Philip Freneau on the Cession of Florida," *Florida Historical Quarterly*, XXI, 40-43, July, 1942).

"The Exile of St. Helena," August 4, September 1 and 15, 1821.

"The Dotage of Royalty," August 11, 1821.

"On National Prospects and Improvements," May 25, 1822.

"The Alleghany Beer-House (Written Several Years Ago) Addressed to a Man in Power," June 8, 1822.

"On the New York Claims to the Exclusive Navigation and Use of the Waters Bounding on the Eastern Coasts of New Jersey As Far As High Water Mark," ·June 15, 1822.

"The Promenade; or, Walks of Art and Nature," June 29, 1822.

"The Female Astrologer (A New England Story)," June 29, 1822.

Stanzas following an account of Eleuthra in the Bahamas, "written on the aforementioned spot in 1786," July 13, 1822.

"The Dying Prophesy of Tecumseh," *Fredonian*, January 30, 1823.

"On the Reign of Peace, and Improvements in Arts, Science, with Some Lines Commemorative of Gen. James J. Wilson, Deceased," August 24, 1824 (reprinted in the *Fredonian*, September 22, 1824).

"On Signora Cachami, the Sicilian Dwarf Lady, About Eighteen and One Quarter Inches in Height; and, for Several Years, Past, Exhibited as a Curiosity, or *Lusus Naturae*, in London," September 4, 1824 (reprinted in the *Fredonian*, September 15, 1824).

"Submarine Taxation. A Voice from the Sea-Coasts of New Jersey," September 11, 1824.

"Extract of a Letter from Cadet George to His Cousin Jonathan," September 25, 1824.

"Lines to the Memory of John Nathan Hutchins, Who, for More Than Fifty Successive Years, Published an Almanac in This Country," *Fredonian*, September 29, 1824.

"A Village Dialogue, between Madam Fly-About and Dorothy Doolittle, Her Female Companion," October 1, 1824.

"The Portrait Painter. On Several Ill Drawn Pictures of Men Celebrated in and Since the Revolutionary War in America, Suspended from the Wall of a Certain Country Hotel, or Tavern," October 16, 1824 (reprinted in the *Fredonian*, November 8, 1824, as "The Groupe. At a Certain Tavern in Long Island, a Number of Celebrated Revolutionary Personages, and Others Are Displayed on a Wall Drawn by a Portrait Painter, by No Means Master of His Business").

"On General La Fayette's Approach to York, in Virginia," October 24, 1824 (reprinted in the *Fredonian*, November 11, 1824).

"Stanzas, Written at a Small House in Chestnut Street, Philadelphia, Occupied Some Years Ago, as a Tavern or Beer House; and Erected by the Famous William Penn About the Year 1769, Being the First House Built on the Spot Where Philadelphia Now Stands," November 13, 1824.

Notes

STANZAS ON THE GREAT COMET

"STANZAS Written in September, 1811, on the great Comet, which had then passed its perihelion, and was travelling rapidly to the southward. To Ismenia," *New-York Weekly Museum,* August 10, 1816, signed "P. F."

THE NEGLECTED HUSBAND

Fredonian, September 5, 1822, dated "Aug. 16, 1822." Reprinted, signed "A.," *True American,* December 28, 1822. First appeared as "On Madam Charity Careless. A Disconsolate Widow," *New-York Weekly Museum,* August 31, 1816, signed "P. F." and with the following variations: introductory lines 1-2, omitted; line 5, "said" for "thought"; line 6, "lived" for "danced" (the *True American* version reads "flirted"); line 7, "he lived or did not" for "he lived or he died" (the *True American* version reads "he fretted or not"); line 9 reads "Poor Richard was out of her thought"; lines 11-18, omitted; line 20, "sat down to his" for "neglected the" (the *True American* version reads "abandoned the"); line 33, "Sally" for "Dolly"; line 43, "at last came" for "came at last"; line 47, "sigh" for "groan"; line 49 reads "Where is it? who knows it?—Not I"; line 50 reads "Only HE who created it, knows"; line 51, "follows" for "follow'd."

STANZAS WRITTEN FOR A LAD

"The following stanzas were written for a lad about eight years of age, who, walking a small distance before his parents through a forest of pine trees, in those solitary deserts, very narrowly escaped being bitten by an uncommonly large and venomous snake of this species. The Serpent, when with some difficulty and risque, killed by the father, measured upward of nine feet in length, and had thirteen rattles on his tail," *True American,* October 12, 1822, signed "E." and dated "August, 1822." First printed in *New-York Weekly Museum,* September 7, 1816, signed "P. F.," as "Stanzas Written for a Boy about eight years of age, who, in walking with his parents through a forest of Pine Trees, very narrowly escaped being bitten by an uncommonly large and venomous Rattle Snake. The Snake, which was killed with some difficulty, measured more than 13 feet long." Reprinted in *Fredonian,* September 12, 1822, signed "F.," as "Lines written for a lad of about eight years of age, who almost miraculously, escaped the bite of an uncommonly large rattlesnake." Lines 9-12 did not appear in the first version; in line 22 "lurking" appeared for "treacherous."

TO MR. BLANCHARD

"Stanzas Addressed several years ago to Mr. Blanchard, the celebrated Aeronaut in America," *New-York Weekly Museum,* September 21, 1816, signed "P. F." For Freneau's reaction to Blanchard's flight in 1793, see Lewis Leary, "Phaeton in Philadelphia," *Pennsylvania Magazine of History and Biography*, XLVII, 49-60 (January, 1943).

THE FORTUNATE BLACKSMITH
  New-York Weekly Museum, September 28, 1816, signed "F."

SALUTARY MAXIMS
  True American, February 8, 1823. First printed, as "Salutary Maxims, Derived from the old Cynic Philosophy," in *New-York Weekly Museum*, October 5, 1816, signed "F." In its earlier form, after line 4 appeared

> Pray to whom or when they will
> On the plain or up the hill:

line 5, "in" for "with"; line 8, *"cross"* for *"mean"*; lines 9-12 omitted; line 15, "Try" for "Strive"; line 18, "will" for "would"; line 21, "girls" for "girl"; lines 23-26 omitted.

STANZAS WRITTEN IN AN ANCIENT BURIAL GROUND
  "Stanzas Written in an ancient Burial Ground, one corner of which has been appropriated to the interments of Suicides," *Fredonian*, February 27, 1823, signed "R." and dated "Feb. 25, 1823." First printed in *New-York Weekly Museum*, October 12, 1816, signed "F.," as "Stanzas Written in an ancient Burying Ground in Maryland, one corner of which was appropriated to the interment of Suicides, or self-murderers." In place of the first two quatrains of the 1823 version, we find in 1816:

> *"When* troubles come and cares perplex
>   (An ancient Roman said)
> Why stay where plagues and sorrows vex?
>   Let's mingle with the dead."—
>
> He should have known, (that Roman old)
>   That cares should rouse the mind
> In life's worst storms to be most bold,
>   At least, to be resign'd.
>
> I say, when plagues and woes distract,
>   When evil days arrive
> 'Tis wrong to do the *fatal act,*
>   'Tis nobler far *to live.*

Other variants in the earlier version: line 10, "Regarded not the sun that beams delight"; line 11, "But, sick of life, explored" for "When life disgust'd, forc'd"; line 14, "That bids us live—that" for "That warms our clay, a"; line 16, "*Here* bound to stay till nature breaks the bands"; line 17, "audacious" for "presumptive"; line 18, "Stricts to thy" for "Aims at the"; line 19, "How will you at that *great tribunal* stand"; line 20, "judged" for "doom'd"; line 21, "human life" for "all our years"; line 22, "we" for "man"; line 23, "When this world's" for " 'Till life's rude"; line 24, "Spring, in its beauty will no doubt appear."

EPITAPH UPON A SPANISH HORSE

"Epitaph Upon a Spanish horse called Royal-Gift, sent over and presented to General Washington by the King of Spain in the year 1785," *New-York Weekly Museum,* October 12, 1816, signed "F."

THE TYE-WIG

"The Tye-Wig. Lines to an old Dotard, who cut away the Blossoms of *Sixty-Eight,* and upwards, to put on a fashionable Tye-Wig," *New-York Weekly Museum,* October 19, 1816, signed "F."

LETITIA

"Letitia: or the Fortunate Spinning Girl," *New-York Weekly Museum,* November 2, 1816, signed "F."

A DIALOGUE

New-York Weekly Museum, November 9, 1816, signed "F."

THE GREAT WESTERN CANAL

"Stanzas on the Great Western Canal of the State of New York," *Fredonian,* August 8, 1822, signed "F." At the end of the poem Freneau noted: "On June 1st 1822 the canal had an uninterrupted navigation of two hundred and twenty eight miles. Then there remained to be finished, about 122 miles to Buffalo, at which place the canal will be connected with Lake Erie. The whole will be completed, it is said, by October 1825.—It is calculated it will then produce an annual revenue of ten millions of dollars! A sum almost exceeding the credibility and transcending the most reasonable computation —as well as sanguine expectation." The poem had appeared as "Stanzas Written on the Grand Western Canal of the State of New York, contemplated to connect the Atlantic Ocean with the interior Lakes of North America," *True American,* June 30, 1821, with an introductory note: "Rejoicing at the progress of Inland Navigation in the State of New York, and delighted at seeing the Muses directing their attention to such patriotic objects, it may well be believed that we give a hearty welcome to the following Communication from a Revolutionary Patriot and Poet." The earlier version contains the following variations: line 13, "begun" for "progress"; lines 14-15 omitted; line 16, "her task was done" for "enlightens man"; lines 19-22 omitted; line 24, "glorious toil" for "unrivalled work"; line 29, "Reason's self" for "*truth*, severe"; lines 43-48 omitted; line 53, "the sail transmits" for "our fleets transport"; line 54, "or" for "and"; line 56, "oceans" for "billows"; line 58, "make" for "bid"; lines 63-64 omitted; line 66, "or" for "and"; lines 67-78 omitted; line 82, "checked" for "changed"; line 84, "Create" for "Conduct," "on" for "through." For a transcript of Freneau's rough manuscript draft of the poem, see Lewis Leary, "Philip Freneau at Seventy," *Journal of the Rutgers University Library*, I, 2-3 (June, 1938).

THE RE-OPENING OF THE PARK THEATRE

"Address, Presented to be spoken at the re-opening of the Park Theatre, in New-York, sometime since destroyed by fire, and now completely repaired and rebuilt in a superior style. Said to be written by P. Freneau, of Monmouth, New-Jersey," *True American*, September 8, 1821. The Park Theatre was destroyed by fire in May, 1820. When the building was repaired a year later, a competition was announced "for the most appropriate and best written Poetic Address" to be spoken on the first night (*New York American*, May 21, 1821). Poems were to be "submitted to a committee of literary gentlemen," and the author of the address selected, if a resident of New York, was to be "entitled to the *freedom of the theatre*; if a resident of any other part of the State or Union, to a Gold Medal of the value of fifty dollars." Sixty poets entered the competition, which was won by Charles Sprague, of Boston, whose prize address was delivered from the stage on the night of September 1, 1821 (*New York Evening Post*, September 2, 1821). At the next performance an "Address written by Mr. [Samuel] Woodworth of this city" (perhaps the second prize poem) was read. (See George C. Odell, *Annals of the New York Stage*, New York, 1927, III, 597.) It may be supposed that the verses which Freneau published in the *True American* represent his unsuccessful contribution to the competition.

JERSEY CITY

"Jersey City. Lines written in a Church-Yard on Bergen Heights, near the village of Hoboken, on the Hudson," *True American*, September 29, 1821.

THE CITY POET

True American. October 6, 1821. The complete poem, in essentially the same form in which it was published, appears in Freneau's autograph on the flyleaf and inside covers of his copy of Benjamin Rush, *Address to the Inhabitants of the British Settlements in America upon Slave-Keeping* (Philadelphia, 1773), in the Princeton University Library, from which it was printed by Varum Lansing Collins, in "A Poem by Philip Freneau, Class of 1771," *Nassau Literary Magazine*, LV, 448-50 (February, 1900).

ELIJAH
True American, October 13, November 3, December 1, and 15, 1821.

TO A YOUNG FRIEND, WITH SOME MAPLE SUGAR
"The following lines were written by a venerable Patriot, who will neither eat, drink, nor wear any thing of a foreign production or manufacture, from a belief that we can raise and make all that we need, and that we ought to give *our own* the preference. They were not written for publication; but we have been permitted to transcribe them by a friend to whom a copy of them was transmitted," *True American,* April 13, 1822, dated "March 13, 1822."

THE YOUTH OF THE MIND
True American, May 11, 1822, signed "F."

PROLOGUE TO KOTZEBUE'S PLAY
"Prologue to Kotzebue's Play, entitled 'The Stranger,' acted for the celebrated Mrs. *Baldwin's* Benefit, at Washington Hall, New-York, April 15, 1822. *Said to be written by P. Freneau, of N. Jersey,*" *True American,* May 18, 1822. Mrs. Baldwin, noted as a tragedian, advertized the benefit in the *New York Evening Post,* April 15, 1822. No playbill of the performance seems to have survived, nor is any mention of a prologue written by Freneau found in the New York newspapers of the day.

THE MILITARY GROUND
"Stanza Written on a visit to a field called, 'The Military Ground,' about one mile and a half to the Southward of Newburg, in the county of Orange, State of New York, where the American army was disbanded by General Washington, nearly forty years ago," *Fredonian,* July 18, 1822, signed "F." and dated "June, 1822." The poem had already appeared, dated "April 22, 1822," in the *True American,* June 8, 1822, without the third stanza of the later version, and with "bounding on" for "hastening to" in the last line of stanza six.

ON THE LOSS OF THE PACKET SHIP ALBION
Fredonian, June 27, 1822. First printed as "On the loss of the ship Albion, Capt. Williams, wrecked near Kinsale Harbor, in Ireland, on the 22d of April last. By Captain Freneau," in both the *True American* and the *New York Statesman* on June 15, 1822, with the following variations: line 5, "bursting" for "boisterous," "Sides" for "flands"; line 7, "In" for "On"; lines 13-18, omitted; line 20, "nigh" for "near"; line 21, "When" for "Where"; line 22, "clear the sky" for "heavens may clear"; line 24, "cheery hearts" for "wind abaft"; line 25, "canvas" for "yards were"; line 28, "pass" for "gain"; line 29, "harbor" for "station"; line 30, "Mersey's" for

"Mercey's"; line 31, "moment" for "instant"; line 33, "skill, or strength" for "power or force"; line 35, "force, no tongue can" for "shock I grieve to"; line 36, "The sails were split" for "Her spars were broke"; line 37, "cried" for "said"; lines 41-42, omitted; line 43, "And" for "Yes"; line 44, "noble ship must" for "gallant Albion"; line 47, "And" for "Our"; line 49, "port" for "friend."

The wreck of the *Albion* was reported in detail by the American press. "No subject for many years has excited poetic sensibility so deeply," said the *True American*, "as the melancholy catastrophe commemorated by Mr. F. with the sympathy of a seaman and the easy skill of a veteran in poesy." "It has awakened the melancholy tones of many a lyre, both in this country and in Europe," reported the *Statesman*, in identifying this poem as by "Capt. Philip Freneau . . . whose patriotic and harmonious pen has amused and interested his country for more than half a century."

To a Young Farmer

"To a young Farmer, or Agriculturist, being taken from the Plough, and sent to College," *True American*, July 6, 1822, signed "R."

To a Young Person Addicted to the Gaming Table

"Stanzas Addressed to a Young Person, of Condition, much addicted to the Gaming Table," *True American*, July 13, 1822, signed "F."

Philosophical Fortitude

Fredonian, July 18, 1822, signed "F."

General Lefevre Denouette

"Stanzas on General Lefevre Denouette, who perished in the wreck of the Albion, April 22, 1822," *Fredonian*, July 25, 1822, signed "F." and dated "July 12, 1822." First printed as "General Lefevre Denouette," *True American*, July 20, 1822, signed "R."

The death of General Denouette is detailed in prose in the *True American*, July 20, 1822: An officer under Napoleon, the general had been for years in exile in the United States. His wife in France had made two unsuccessful attempts to join him. "At length, weary of solitude and situation he determined at every risque, to revisit his native country, and throw himself on the mercy of the king." The intercession of his friends and the "urgent remonstrances of his wife, prevailed so far with the Government, that he was invited to proceed to Holland, to await a speedy compliance to his wishes, to be restored to his country and family. In this expectation, he embarked in the Albion at New-York, and . . . found a watery grave on the coast of Ireland."

ON THE CIVILIZATION OF THE WESTERN ABORIGINAL COUNTRY
True American, July 20, 1822, signed "A."

LINES WRITTEN AT DEMAREST'S FIELD
"Lines written at Demarest's field, near Tappan, on the disinterment and transportation of Major Andre's Bones to England, 1821," *True American,* August 24, 1822, signed "R."

VERSES WRITTEN ON LEAVING A GREAT HOUSE
Fredonian, September 2, 1822, signed "R." and dated "July, 1822." First printed as "Lines, written on leaving an elegant new mansion House, called Beaurepaire (pleasant retreat) not an hundred miles from Lake Cayuga," *True American,* August 24, 1822, signed "N." and dated "May 20, 1822." The earlier version contained the following variants: line 7, "trim" for "comb," "dust" for brush"; lines 13-24, omitted; line 35, "master" for "giant"; line 36, "deign" for "wish"; line 43, "turned" for "changed"; line 54, "call" for "halt"; line 57, "Indian" for "buckwheat."

VERSES ON AN UPPER STREET PHYSICIAN
"Verses on an Upper Street Physician Who Deserted a Populous City on the Approach of Malignant Fever," *Fredonian,* August 29, 1822. Reprinted, signed "R.," as "Verses on a Physician who deserted a great Commercial City on the approach and symptoms of the yellow or Malignant Fever," *True American,* December 28, 1822.

LINES TO A LADY
"Lines to a Lady Engaged in manufacturing an elegant superfine Carpet, intended to be forwarded, as a present, to Nadir Shah, despot of Persia," *True American,* August 31, 1822, signed "E." and dated "August 2, 1822."

THE PASSAICK GARDEN
"The Passaick Garden, in Essex County, July, 1820," *Fredonian,* October 17, 1822, signed "E." A shorter version of the poem, entitled "Lines written near an elegant and romantic Garden adjacent to Passaick River, in Essex county," appeared in *True American,* September 7, 1822, signed "A.," dated "July, 1822," and with the following variants: line 1, "noon of day or dead of" for "sun or star by day or"; lines 3-4 omitted; line 13, "here be pleased to" for "through this magic"; lines 29-42 omitted; lines 57-58 omitted; line 65, "the" for "a."

BONAPARTE
"The following verses were written at the time the intelligence first arrived in America that Bonaparte, from the first consulship, had ascended the throne of France," *True American,* September 14, 1822, signed "E."

A MIDNIGHT STORM IN THE GULPH STREAM

"A Midnight Storm in the Gulph Stream. Written on an outward *bound voyage from* Charleston to the Canary Islands," *Fredonian,* September 19, 1822, signed "E."; reprinted, signed "F." and dated "Brig Washington, January 25, 1804," *True American,* September 21, 1822.

TO A LADY REMARKABLY FOND OF SLEEP

"Stanzas addressed to a Lady remarkably fond of sleep, preparing for a voyage to Europe from Philadelphia," *Fredonian,* October 5, 1822, signed "R." and dated "Sept. 12." The poem had appeared, signed "A." and dated "September 20, 1822," in the *True American,* September 21, 1822, with a few verbal variations and with the order of stanzas changed to 1, 2, 3, 4, 12, 13, 11, 5, 6, 7, 8, 9, 10, stanza 14 omitted, 15, 16.

THE ARRIVAL AT INDIAN SAM'S

Fredonian, September 26, 1822, signed "E." Reprinted as "The arrival at Wee-guali's or Indian Sam's Wigwam," *True American,* September 28, 1822, signed "N."

CIRCUMNAVIGATION

"Circumnavigation. The United States' Seventy-four gun ship Franklin is now in the Pacific Ocean, supposed to be on a voyage round the Globe. The commanding officer has his Lady with him, which gave occasion to the following lines," *True American,* October 19, 1822, signed "E." and dated "September, 1822."

ODE ON A REMOTE PERSPECTIVE VIEW OF PRINCETON COLLEGE

"Ode on a remote Perspective view of Princeton College, or Nassau Hall, from a remarkable woody Eminence in Monmouth county, called by the neighborhood, Pine Hill," *Fredonian,* October 31, 1822, signed "N.R." and dated "Sept. 25th 1822." The poem had appeared, signed "R." in the *True American,* October 26, 1822. Variants between the two versions will be found in Rudolf Kirk, "Freneau's 'View' of Princeton," *Journal of the Rutgers University Library,* III, 22-25 (December, 1939). I have reprinted, with his permission, Dr. Kirk's admirably edited version.

A TRANSIENT VIEW OF MONTICELLO

"Lines on a Transient View of Monticello, in Virginia," *Fredonian,* November 7, 1822, signed "E." and dated "October, 1822."

ON OBSERVING A LARGE RED-STREAK APPLE

Fredonian, November 14, 1822, signed "E." The poem had appeared, signed "R.," in the *True American,* November 9, 1822, as "On the continuance of a Red-Streak apple on the Tree in the month of January," with the following variations: line 1, "snows" for "snow"; line 2, "every" for "all the," "blows" for "blow"; line 3, "nipping" for "biting"; line 4, "there" for "here"; line 7, "In such a season" for "Amidst this system"; line 14, "one" for "a"; line 15, "finished" for "buried"; line 16, "been" for "have"; line 17, " 'till the future" for "to another"; line 20, "their" for "the"; line 21, "haste" for "get"; line 30, "youthful bloom" for "bloom of youth"; after line 30

> I would those wrinkles smooth again,
> And blood renew in every vein;

line 31, "redress" for "restrain"; line 32, "with another summer bless" for "bring your blossom state again"; line 36, "we" for "I"; line 40, "I" for "we"; line 46, "summer-time" for "summers time."

A FRAGMENT OF BION

"Translated from a fragment of Bion, an ancient Grecian philosopher and poet," *Fredonian*, November 28, 1822, signed "R." At the end of the poem Freneau notes: "The preceding lines, in the original, were written by Bion, a celebrated pagan philosopher of Smyrna, in the Lesser Asia, and commonly classed among the minor Greek Poets. He is very ancient, and not long after the time of Homer. From the few fragments of his writings that remain, it appears he believed that the soul and body died together.—Yet, it is remarkable, he here declares that if he could persuade himself, there was to be a future state of happiness, he should think no diligence or pains too much to be partaker of that eternal inheritance. What a lesson to the professors of Christianity, from the pen of a mere moralist, a child of nature and hedonism!" Lines 15-26, 31-32, had been published by Freneau years before, in the *National Gazette*, October 16, 1793, with the following variations: line 16, "successive" for "succeeding"; for lines 21-22

> No task too hard, too rough no road
> That led to that serene abode—

line 32, "each delight is pall'd by" for "every sense declines with."

ANSWER TO A LETTER OF DESPONDENCY

"Answer to a letter of despondency from an Invalid in the North," *True American*, February 8, 1823, signed "R. R." A version only very slightly different, which appeared, over the signature "F." and dated "Long Branch, November 20," in the *Fredonian*, December 5, 1822, has been reprinted by Lewis Leary in "Philip Freneau at Seventy," *Journal of the Rutgers University Library*, I, 11-13 (June, 1938). Freneau's correspondent may have been his sister Margaret Hunn or his unmarried sister Mary, both of whom were at this time over sixty and living in Newburgh, New York. The similarity of these verses to those of Pope in "To Mr. C. of St. James Place" has already been remarked.

To a New-England Poet
   True American, January 4, 1823, signed "N."

On a Widow Lady
   True American, February 1, 1823, signed "R."

On the Death of Robert Fulton
   "Lines Written several years ago on the death of Robert Fulton, (who departed this life in February, 1815), the celebrated mechanical philosopher, the *Archimedes* of America, who by his inventions, discoveries, and improvements in machinery, acted upon by *aquatic steam,* introduced a new system of river and coast navigation, for which the civilized world at large, and North America in particular, should pay that respect to his memory, which is all that a distinguished and really useful character is generally allowed to receive.—It may not be known to every one that Fulton's body was deposited in the Livingston family vault, at *Clermont,* near the margin of Hudson's River," *True American,* February 1, 1823, signed "E." and dated "June, 1816."

General De la Fayette
   Fredonian, August 18, 1824, signed "F." and dated "Shrewsbury Beach, June 25, 1824." First printed in *True American,* July 31, 1824, with the following variations: lines 54-57, omitted; line 59, "The starry" for "Columbia's"; lines 60-63, omitted; for line 64, "And there in golden letters sit"; line 65, the word "For" omitted.

Stanzas Made at the Interment of a Sailor
   "Stanzas Made at the interment of a Sailor on the island of Tortuga, near the north side of Hispaniola, or Hayti, as now called. (Written many years ago, but never published)," *True American,* August 24, 1824, signed "F." Appeared as "Stanzas, Made at the interring of a Sailor . . . ," *Fredonian,* September 8, 1824, with the following variants: line 19, "sphere" for "globe"; lines 29-36, omitted.

Winter
   This is the last of Freneau's poems which has been discovered. It exists only in manuscript, dated "November 28, 1827," in the New York Public Library.